12 DAYS OF CHRISTMAS

with

Six Sisters' STUFF

12 DAYS OF CHRISTMAS

with

Six Sisters' STUFF

144 IDEAS FOR TRADITIONS, HOMEMADE GIFTS, RECIPES, AND MORE

SHADOW
MOUNTAIN

TO ALL OUR READERS AND

ESPECIALLY OUR FAVORITE LITTLE

FOLLOWERS, OUR CHILDREN

All photographs courtesy SixSistersStuff.com.

Except for the following photographs: page 24 © Eanpictures/Shutterstock.com (weights); page 24 © Timmary/Shutterstock.com (sushi); page 25 © Dan Thornberg/Shutterstock.com (clock); page 25 © Edyta Pawlowska/Shutterstock.com (music); page 25 © Goodluz/Shutterstock.com (writing); page 25 © Lilyana Vynogradova/Shutterstock.com (donuts); page 26 © Arina P Habich/Shutterstock.com (house); page 28 © Elena Shashkina/Shutterstock.com (hot chocolate); page 54 © wavebreakmedia/Shutterstock.com (Christmas tree); page 55 © pogonici/Shutterstock.com (piggy bank); page 55 © Tish1/Shutterstock.com (wrapping paper); page 55 © Ronald Sumners/Shutterstock.com (slow-cooker); page 56 © mangostock/Shutterstock.com (donation box); page 57 © Fotyma/Shutterstock.com (game); page 57 © Pressmaster/Shutterstock.com (family); page 60 © Jenn Huls/Shutterstock.com (presents).

Visit us at ShadowMountain.com

Library of Congress Cataloging-in-Publication Data

12 days of Christmas with Six Sisters' Stuff : 144 Ideas for traditions, homemade gifts, recipes, and more / Six Sisters' Stuff.
  pages cm
Includes index.
  Summary: Compilation of more than 144 Christmas recipes, traditions, and craft ideas that celebrate family and the holiday.
  ISBN 978-1-60907-935-2 (paperbound)
  1. Christmas cooking. 2. Christmas decorations. 3. Christmas. 4. Gifts. 5. Handicraft. I. Six Sisters, issuing body.
GT4985.A22 2014
394.2663–dc23   2014019064

Printed in Canada
Friesens, Manitoba, Canada

10 9 8 7 6 5 4 3 2 1

CONTENTS

12 CHRISTMAS COOKIES

Holiday Sprinkle Cookies 1

Santa Sugar Cookies 2

Cherry Cheesecake Cookies 5

Eggnog Cookies 6

Andes Mint Grinch Cookies 9

Chocolate Orange Cookies 10

Chocolate Chip Turtle Cookies 13

Soft and Chewy Molasses Cookies 15

Frosted Toffee Cookies 16

Mint Chip Cookies 18

Grandma's Thumbprint Cookies 21

Gooey Butter Cookies 22

**12 DAYS OF CHRISTMAS
FOR YOUR TRUE LOVE** 24

12 FAMILY TRADITIONS 26

12 CHRISTMAS BRUNCH RECIPES

Bacon and Egg Breakfast Casserole 31

Homemade Orange Rolls (with glaze) 32

Baked Apple Pie French Toast 35

Gingerbread Waffles 36

Warm Spiced Cider 39

Nutella Banana Bread 40

Gooey Caramel Pull-Aparts 43

Homemade French Toast Sticks 44

Cherry Chocolate Muffins 47

Eggs a la Goldenrod 48

Brunch Enchiladas 51

Homemade Waffles with
    Chocolate-Hazelnut Sauce 52

**12 SANITY-SAVING
CHRISTMAS TIPS** 54

12 CHRISTMAS PARTY IDEAS 58

12 SPECTACULAR CHRISTMAS TREATS

Gingerbread Cookie Bars 67

Peanut Butter Snowballs 68

Double-Decker Fudge 71

Pumpkin Pie Cake 72

Almond English Toffee 75

Eggnog Gingerbread Trifle 76

Peppermint Crunch Ice Cream Pie 79

Dutch Apple Pie 81

Almond Joy Bars 82

Peppermint Fudge 84

Baby Ruth Bars 87

Mini Turtle Cheesecakes 88

12 WAYS TO GIVE BACK 90

12 GIFTS FOR NEIGHBORS 94

12 QUICK AND EASY FAMILY DINNERS

Slow-Cooker Ham with Honey Mustard Glaze 99

Slow-Cooker Ham and Pineapple Sandwiches 100

Slow-Cooker Balsamic Pot Roast 103

Slow-Cooker Chicken and Gravy 104

Slow-Cooker Chicken Fajita Soup 107

Slow-Cooker Texas Chili 109

Citrus-Glazed Salmon 110

Applesauce Pork Tenderloin 112

Sticky Sesame Chicken 115

Grandma's Meatloaf 116

Perfect Fried Pork Chops 119

Chicken Taco Casserole 120

12 HOMEMADE CHRISTMAS GIFTS

Glass Vase Christmas Luminaries 122

T-Shirt Superhero Cape 123

Burlap Handprint Tree Skirt 124

Personalized Books on CD 125

Wood Photo Blocks 126

DIY Bleach T-Shirts 127

Easy Infinity Scarf 128

Hinge Bracelet 128

T-Shirt Headband 130

Recipe Binder 131

Photo Clock 131

Magnetic Birthday Calendar 132

12 DIY CHRISTMAS DECORATIONS

Cinnamon Stick Candles 134

DIY Wood Candle Holders 135

Peppermint Candy Wreath 136

Sequin Christmas Tree 136

Christmas Card Holder 137

Christmas Countdown Advent Calendar 138

Candy Cane Frame 139

Merry Christmas Canvas 140

Polka Dot Burlap Table Runner 140

Christmas Monogram Hanging 141

Fabric-Covered Decorative Books 142

Christmas Ornament Garland 143

INDEX 145

MERRY CHRISTMAS
from Six Sisters' Stuff

Holiday Sprinkle Cookies

These cute cookies look like donut holes cut in half and filled with delicious icing. In reality, they are soft cookies loaded with fun sprinkles. Fun and festive, they are a great addition to any holiday party.

⅔ cup butter, softened	1 teaspoon vanilla
½ cup granulated sugar	1¼ cups all-purpose flour
¼ cup unsweetened cocoa powder	1 cup rainbow sprinkles, such as Wilton's Rainbow Jimmies
¼ teaspoon baking soda	1 recipe Simple Frosting
⅛ teaspoon salt	
1 large egg	

In a large bowl, beat butter on medium speed until creamy. Add sugar, cocoa powder, baking soda, and salt. Mix well until combined. Mix in the egg and vanilla. Slowly beat in flour. Finished dough should not be sticky.

Fill a small bowl with rainbow sprinkles. Roll dough into 24 one-inch balls and then roll in the sprinkles until completely coated. Place sprinkle-coated dough balls on greased baking sheets and refrigerate 15 minutes. Bake at 375 degrees F. for 8 to 10 minutes. Don't overcook; the tops should not crack. While cookies are baking, prepare the frosting.

To assemble cookies, spread frosting on 1 cookie and top with a second cookie to make a sandwich. Repeat with remaining cookies. These cookies are good to eat without frosting too! Makes 12 sandwich cookies

SIMPLE FROSTING

½ cup butter, softened	1 teaspoon vanilla
1½ cups powdered sugar	

In a large bowl, beat together butter and powdered sugar on low speed. Add vanilla and beat on high speed until light and fluffy.

Santa Sugar Cookies

Frosting sugar cookies is a family tradition. One year, Mom saw some darling Santa cookies at a local bakery and decided she could easily make her own. Her first attempt was a huge hit at our holiday party.

1 cup butter or margarine, softened*	4 cups all-purpose flour
1¼ cups granulated sugar	1 recipe Buttercream Frosting
2 eggs	Red sugar crystals, for Santa's hat
1 teaspoon vanilla	Sweetened flaked coconut, for Santa's beard
1 teaspoon baking powder	Chocolate chips, for Santa's eyes
1 teaspoon baking soda	Cinnamon Red Hots, for Santa's nose
½ teaspoon salt	Miniature marshmallows, for the pom-pom on Santa's hat
½ cup sour cream	

Preheat oven to 350 degrees F.

In a large bowl, cream together butter or margarine, sugar, and eggs until well blended. Add vanilla, baking powder, baking soda, salt, and sour cream and stir well. Add flour and gently combine. If dough seems too sticky, add just a little more flour and refrigerate 30 minutes. (If dough is not sticky, there is no need to refrigerate.) On a well-floured surface, roll out dough to ¼-inch thickness. Cut dough into circles with a 2¾-inch round cookie cutter (the diameter can be a little more or less if you don't have this precise size). Bake on ungreased cookie sheets about 9 minutes, until they are set, barely golden on the edge (you don't want to overcook them!). Remove cookies to a wire rack to cool.

To make Santa's face, decorate cookies one at a time so the frosting does not have time to harden before sprinkling on sugar crystals and coconut. Spread Buttercream Frosting over the entire cookie. Gently place a small bowl over the bottom two-thirds of the cookie. Sprinkle the uncovered portion of the cookie with red sugar crystals. Remove the bowl and sprinkle coconut over the bottom third of the cookie, coming up a little on each side to meet the hat. This will be Santa's beard and should leave you with a small frosting-only area for Santa's face. Use 2 chocolate chips to make Santa's eyes and 1 cinnamon red hot for his nose. Place 1 miniature marshmallow on the left or right side, where Santa's hat and beard meet.

Makes 4 dozen cookies.

*Using margarine will give you softer and fluffier cookies. Butter tends to make a flatter cookie.

BUTTERCREAM FROSTING

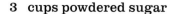

3	tablespoons shortening	3	cups powdered sugar
½	cup butter or margarine, melted		
1	teaspoon vanilla		
1	tablespoon milk		

In a medium bowl, beat together shortening and butter or margarine until smooth. Mix in vanilla and milk. Add powdered sugar and mix on medium speed until light and fluffy. If frosting seems too thin, add more powdered sugar; if it's too thick, add a little more milk.

Cherry Cheesecake Cookies

Cheesecake in the form of a cookie? Brilliant! These cookies have been winners at two different cookie contests. Not only are they cute to look at, but they also taste absolutely amazing. It just wouldn't be Christmas without them!

½ cup butter, softened

1 (3-ounce) package cream cheese, room temperature

1 egg, separated

1 teaspoon vanilla

1 teaspoon lemon zest

¼ teaspoon salt

1 cup powdered sugar

1 cup all-purpose flour

1 cup graham cracker crumbs (about 5 whole graham crackers)

1 (20-ounce) can cherry pie filling

In a medium bowl, cream together butter, cream cheese, egg yolk, vanilla, lemon zest, and salt until light and fluffy. Gradually mix in powdered sugar and then the flour to make stiff dough. Cover bowl with plastic wrap and place in the refrigerator to chill about 2 hours.

Remove dough from fridge and preheat oven to 325 degrees F.

Shape dough into 1-inch balls. In a shallow bowl beat egg white until foamy. Place graham cracker crumbs in a separate shallow bowl. Dip dough balls in egg white then roll in graham cracker crumbs. Arrange cookie dough balls about 2 inches apart on ungreased cookie sheet. Using your thumb, make a depression in the middle of each cookie.

Bake 12 to 15 minutes, until cookies begin to brown on the bottoms. Remove cookies from baking sheet and let cool. Fill depression with 1 teaspoon pie filling (or as much as you can fit on each cookie).

Makes about 30 cookies.

Eggnog Cookies

One of the many reasons we love this time of year is the eggnog! When we were little, eggnog was a special treat. We didn't have it often, but when we did, we savored every sip! These cookies have just the right amount of eggnog flavor. Even your eggnog-haters might change their minds about the drink with these cookies!

1¼ cups granulated sugar	2¼ cups all-purpose flour
1 cup butter, at room temperature, divided	1 teaspoon baking powder
1 teaspoon vanilla	½ teaspoon cinnamon
2 egg yolks	½ teaspoon nutmeg
1 cup light eggnog, divided	3 cups powdered sugar

Preheat oven to 300 degrees F.

In a large bowl, cream together sugar and ¾ cup of the butter with an electric mixer. Add vanilla, egg yolks, and ½ cup of the eggnog. Beat at medium speed until smooth.

In a medium bowl, whisk together flour, baking powder, cinnamon, and nutmeg; add dry mixture to wet ingredients and stir well. Cover dough with plastic wrap and chill in refrigerator 30 minutes to 1 hour.

Drop chilled dough by rounded teaspoons onto greased baking sheets, 1 to 2 inches apart. Bake 17 to 22 minutes, or until bottoms turn light brown. Immediately transfer cookies to wire racks to prevent them from further baking on the hot cookie sheet.

Once cookies are cooled, prepare icing in a small mixing bowl. Beat the powdered sugar and remaining ¼ cup butter until well blended. Gradually beat in remaining ½ cup eggnog until icing reaches desired consistency. If you prefer a thicker icing, use less eggnog and frost the cookies with a flat spatula; if you prefer a thin icing, use more eggnog and drizzle the icing over cookies with a spoon. Let the icing harden before serving.

Makes about 36 cookies.

Andes Mint Grinch Cookies

A bright green color and a minty flavor make a wonderful combination for a cookie! These would be great for a cookie swap or for a fun treat to eat while watching Dr. Seuss' *How the Grinch Stole Christmas!*

½ cup butter, at room temperature

½ cup shortening

1½ cups granulated sugar

2 eggs

1 teaspoon mint extract

3 cups all-purpose flour

2 teaspoons baking powder

1 teaspoon baking soda

½ teaspoon salt

15 to 20 drops green food coloring

1 cup Andes Crème De Menthe Baking Chips

Preheat oven 375 degrees F.

In a large bowl, cream together butter, shortening, and sugar until smooth. Beat in eggs and mint extract. In a separate bowl, sift together flour, baking powder, baking soda, and salt. Gradually blend dry ingredients into wet ingredients. Add the green food coloring and mix until coloring is even. Fold in the Andes baking chips. Cover dough with plastic wrap and chill in the refrigerator 30 minutes to an hour.

Roll chilled dough into 1-inch balls and place them on ungreased cookie sheets, about 2 inches apart. Bake 8 to 10 minutes. Let cookies stand on baking sheets 2 minutes before moving them to wire racks to cool.

Makes 36 cookies.

Chocolate Orange Cookies

Growing up, we always got a chocolate orange in our stockings on Christmas morning. These cookies are reminiscent of that fabulous chocolate and orange flavor combination. Plus, they are really easy to make but taste like you spent all day in the kitchen!

1 (15.25-ounce) box milk chocolate cake mix

2 eggs

⅓ cup vegetable oil

1¼ cups butter, at room temperature, divided

2 tablespoons milk

2 to 3 cups powdered sugar

1½ teaspoons orange extract

Red and yellow food coloring (optional)

2¼ cups semisweet chocolate chips

Preheat oven to 350 degrees F.

In a large bowl, add cake mix, eggs, and vegetable oil. Stir until well combined. Roll dough into 1-inch balls and place on ungreased cookie sheets. Bake 6 to 8 minutes, until cookies are puffed and set. Remove from baking sheets and let cool completely.

Prepare orange buttercream filling in a medium bowl by beating ½ cup of the butter until smooth. Slowly add milk and then powdered sugar and beat until fluffy. Stir in orange extract. If desired add a few drops of red and yellow food coloring to turn the frosting orange. Let the frosting set for 10 minutes, then spread a generous amount of frosting on each cookie.

Melt chocolate chips and the remaining ¾ cup butter in the microwave for 2 minutes, stirring halfway through. Mix until smooth and spread over orange frosted cookies.

Makes 36 cookies.

Chocolate Chip Turtle Cookies

There's nothing like homemade chocolate chip cookies, especially when topped with creamy caramel and pecans. This is a delicious twist on the chocolate chip cookie that your family is bound to love!

2½ cups all-purpose flour

1 teaspoon baking soda

1 teaspoon salt

1 cup butter, at room temperature

⅔ cup granulated sugar

⅔ cup packed brown sugar

1 teaspoon vanilla

2 large eggs

2 cups milk chocolate chips

14 squares Kraft Caramels, unwrapped

3 tablespoons heavy cream

½ cup chopped pecans

Preheat oven to 375 degrees F.

Combine flour, baking soda, and salt in a small bowl; set aside. In a large bowl beat butter, sugars, and vanilla until creamy. Add eggs, one at a time, beating well after each addition. Gradually beat in flour mixture. Fold in chocolate chips. Drop by rounded tablespoon onto ungreased baking sheets. Bake 9 to 11 minutes, or until golden brown. Let cookies cool completely.

In a small bowl, microwave caramels and cream 1 to 2 minutes on high power, stirring occasionally, until smooth. Drizzle caramel mixture over cookies and sprinkle with chopped pecans.

Makes 48 cookies.

Soft and Chewy Molasses Cookies

This is *the* perfect soft ginger cookie and a great treat for the holiday season!

2¼ cups all-purpose flour

2 teaspoons ground ginger

1 teaspoon baking soda

¾ teaspoon ground cinnamon

½ teaspoon ground cloves

¼ teaspoon salt

¾ cup butter or margarine, softened

1 cup granulated sugar, plus more for coating

1 egg

1 tablespoon water

¼ cup molasses

Preheat oven to 350 degrees F.

Sift together flour, ginger, baking soda, cinnamon, cloves, and salt. Set aside.

In a large bowl, cream together margarine and 1 cup sugar until light and fluffy. Beat in egg. Stir in the water and molasses.

Add about ¼ cup sugar to a shallow bowl. Shape dough into 1-inch balls and roll in sugar. Place dough balls 2 inches apart on ungreased cookie sheets. Slightly flatten each ball. Bake 8 to 10 minutes. Allow cookies to cool on baking sheet 5 minutes before removing to wire rack.

Makes about 36 cookies.

Frosted Toffee Cookies

Christmastime is exciting and magical. As kids, we loved coming home from a fun evening out and finding Christmas goodies on the porch from neighbors and friends. These frosted toffee cookies are perfect for your neighbor goody plates.

½ cup butter or margarine, softened

½ cup brown sugar

½ teaspoon vanilla

1 egg

1¾ cups flour

¼ teaspoon salt

¼ teaspoon baking soda

⅔ cup chocolate toffee bits (about 3 Heath or Skor bars, crushed) divided

1 recipe Toffee Glaze

⅓ cup semisweet chocolate chips

⅓ cup white chocolate chips

½ teaspoon vegetable oil, divided

Preheat oven to 325 degrees F.

In a large bowl beat together butter, brown sugar, vanilla, and egg on medium speed until light and fluffy. Switch mixer to low speed and mix in flour, salt, and baking soda. Set aside ⅓ of the toffee bits for garnishing. Stir remaining toffee bits into the cookie dough. Roll dough into 1-inch balls and place on ungreased cookie sheets about 1 inch apart.

Bake 10 to 12 minutes, or until tops of cookies feel set when touched. Remove cookies to wire racks to cool.

Once cookies are cooled, prepare Toffee Glaze. Cover the top of each cookie with the glaze.

Place chocolate chips and white chips in separate microwavable bowls. Add ¼ teaspoon vegetable oil to each bowl. Microwave on high 1 to 1½ minutes, stirring every 30 seconds, until melted. Using the tip of a spoon, lightly drizzle melted chocolate and melted white chocolate over each cookie. Sprinkle with remaining toffee bits. Let cookies set up before serving. For quicker setting, chill in the refrigerator.

Makes 24 cookies.

TOFFEE GLAZE

¼ **cup butter or margarine**

½ **cup brown sugar**

3 **tablespoons milk**

1⅓ **cups powdered sugar**

Heat butter, brown sugar, and milk over medium-low heat in a 1-quart saucepan. Stir frequently until mixture just comes to a boil and sugar is dissolved. Stir in powdered sugar and beat until smooth.

Mint Chip Cookies

If you're looking for the perfect cookies to leave out for Santa, these are the ones to pile on a plate. This chocolate cookie almost has the texture of a brownie: perfectly chewy on the outside and soft on the inside.

⅔ cup shortening

1 cup packed brown sugar

½ cup granulated sugar

2 eggs

1 teaspoon vanilla

1 tablespoon water

1½ cups all-purpose flour

⅓ cup unsweetened cocoa powder

¼ teaspoon baking soda

½ teaspoon salt

2 cups green mint chips

Preheat oven to 375 degrees F.

In a large bowl, cream together shortening and sugars with an electric mixer. Add eggs, one at a time, mixing well in between eggs. Mix in vanilla and water. In a separate bowl, whisk together flour, cocoa powder, baking soda, and salt. Stir flour mixture into creamed mixture until just blended; fold in mint chips. Drop dough by rounded teaspoons 2 inches apart onto ungreased baking sheets.

Bake 7 to 9 minutes. Cool 2 minutes on baking sheets and then transfer cookies to wire racks to cool completely.

Makes about 2 dozen cookies.

Grandma's Thumbprint Cookies

Our Grandma is well known for her delicious Thumbprint Cookies. She always made them with red and green frosting; but if you aren't a frosting fan, you can fill them with your favorite jam or jelly.

½ cup butter, softened

½ cup shortening

½ cup brown sugar

2 eggs, separated

1 teaspoon vanilla

2 cups all-purpose flour

1 teaspoon salt

3 cups finely chopped nuts, such as walnuts or pecans

1½ cups your favorite frosting, jam, or jelly

Preheat oven to 350 degrees F.

In a large bowl, cream together butter, shortening, brown sugar, egg yolks, and vanilla.

Slowly mix in the flour and salt. Shape the dough into 1-inch balls.

In a shallow bowl, beat egg whites until frothy. Add nuts to a separate shallow bowl. Dredge each dough ball in the egg whites then roll in the chopped nuts to coat. Place dough balls 1 inch apart on ungreased cookie sheets. Use your thumb to make a deep imprint in the center of each cookie. If using jam or jelly to fill the thumbprints, spoon 1½ teaspoons in each cookie before baking.

Bake 10 minutes, or until light brown. Immediately remove from cookie sheet to cool. If using frosting to fill thumbprints, spoon 1½ teaspoons in each cookie once cooled.

Makes 48 cookies.

Gooey Butter Cookies

Any cookie that involves cream cheese *and* a cake mix has to be delicious, and this recipe definitely doesn't disappoint. These are the perfect cookies to take to a family gathering, holiday party, or to leave for Santa on Christmas Eve! They take just a few minutes to throw together and taste amazing.

1   (8-ounce) package cream cheese, softened

½   cup butter, softened

1   egg

¼   teaspoon vanilla

1   (16.5-ounce) box yellow cake mix

¼   cup powdered sugar

Preheat oven to 350 degrees F.

In a medium bowl, cream together cream cheese and butter until smooth. Beat in the egg and vanilla. Slowly add the cake mix, blending until well combined. Roll dough into 1-inch balls. Place powdered sugar in a shallow bowl and roll the dough balls in the powdered sugar. Place dough balls 1-inch apart on ungreased cookie sheets. Bake 10 to 13 minutes.

Makes 24 cookies.

12

DAYS OF

CHRISTMAS

for Your True Love

The holiday season always feels so rushed! It's easy to get caught up in the baking, the party-planning, and the shopping, and thus overlook the most important people in your life. We want to remedy that by sharing some great ideas for a Twelve-Days-of-Christmas Countdown for the "True Love" in your life—whether your love is a spouse, friend, child, neighbor, sibling, or parent. Take a step back from the busyness of the season and let your true love know how much you appreciate them!

Day 1: This day is the easiest because you just need one item. Be as creative as you'd like! Think about what your true love likes or needs—a hat, a scarf, a pocket knife, a wallet, headphones, duct tape, or a new basketball.

Day 2: Lots of things come in pairs. Try gloves, tickets to a movie or sporting event, lighters, weights, camping chairs, or a new pair of shoes.

Day 3: Packs of three are also relatively easy to find. Golf balls, tennis balls, movie or book trilogies, socks, packs of gum, or hand warmers all come in packages of three.

Day 4: Packs of four are common too! Snack packs, razor blade refills, pens, Pop-Tarts, or Post-it Notes are always a great idea.

Day 5: This one is simple but fun! Purchase a $5 gift card to your true love's favorite fast-food joint.

Day 6: Candy bars, cupcakes, ice cream treats, soda pop, granola bars, and lunch-sized sushi all come in packs or boxes of six. Take a look down the snack or candy aisle, and you'll definitely find something for your true love.

Day 7: It's a little harder to come up with a pack of seven, so think of the number as a time! Surprise your true love at 7 a.m. with their favorite breakfast or at 7 p.m. with a favorite dessert.

Do anything to make that time of day special! You could even give your true love a simple card with a hand-written love note at that time.

Day 8: Homemade coupons are fun to make and receive! You can include coupons for one free foot massage, a back rub, or one hour of uninterrupted TV.

Day 9: Make a playlist! Choose nine songs from the year you met; nine songs from the year your true love was born; or nine songs that make you think of them.

Day 10: This is another great day for a gift card. iTunes, Amazon, Walmart, Target, and most food places will let you purchase a $10 gift card.

Day 11: Make a list of eleven reasons why you love them. Think about the little things they do that they may not realize but that you love!

Day 12: Lots of things come in dozens! Try giving your true love a twelve-month subscription to a favorite magazine. Tools, rolls, donuts, and soda pop often come in twelve packs as well. If you're feeling creative, use an online photo service to make a calendar for the upcoming year. Use photos of the two of you together throughout the years.

12

FAMILY

TRADITIONS

Traditions are a great way to bring your family together during the holidays. For us, our family traditions were something we looked forward to every Christmas, and something we talked about the whole year through. Whether you do one or all of them, these 12 traditions will help bring your family together this Christmas.

1. BOOK ADVENT
From Kristen

I love advent calendars. Growing up we always had one of those store-bought advent calendars with the chocolates in them! It gave me something to look forward to each day and made Christmas come just a little bit quicker.

To start a Book Advent, I headed to a local thrift store and dug through all their books. Children's books can be expensive, but paying only 50 cents per book was a little easier on my wallet. I found 23 fun Christmas books and came home and wrapped them. Starting on December 1, we unwrapped a book each night and read it together as a family, sitting around our Christmas tree. On the last night—December 24—we read the Christmas story from the Bible.

2. HOLIDAY LIGHT WALK
From Steph

One of my favorite things about the holidays is all the glowing lights. Our annual holiday light walk was always one of my favorite occasions. We would bundle up in lots of layers and head outside to see all the beautiful, twinkling lights around our neighborhood. If there was freshly fallen snow, we would take sleds and our parents would pull some of us behind them. It was a great time to get a little fresh air, spend time together, and enjoy the sights of the season.

3. GINGERBREAD HOUSE CONTEST
From Kendra

I love the smell of gingerbread cooking during the holiday season. One of my favorite traditions was decorating gingerbread houses as a family and listening to Christmas music as we decorated them. As we grew older and our family expanded, we had to make more gingerbread

houses and it turned into a gingerbread house decorating contest. Our family eventually grew so big that we started making our gingerbread houses out of graham crackers. This added to the level of competition, as houses had multiple levels, and our creativity expanded.

4. **ORNAMENT EXCHANGE**
From Kendra

We started this tradition a few years back when my sister heard about another family of sisters who started the tradition. We all go pick out an ornament, wrap it up, then go out to dinner to exchange them. We usually draw numbers to decide who picks first. Sometimes the ornaments are cute; other times, they are just funny. It's a fun tradition we all look forward to.

5. **REINDEER FOOD**
From Lauren

Every Christmas Eve when we were growing up, our mom would make a batch of delicious

cookies to leave out for Santa. One Christmas we decided as sisters that we should probably start leaving something for the reindeer too! And that's when our mom started making Reindeer Food. She would mix together oats and Christmas sprinkles, and we would each get to sprinkle a handful of the colorful mixture on the lawn. The colorful sprinkles would turn the snow green and red, and by the time we woke up it looked as though animals had certainly enjoyed our snack! We were able to sleep much better on Christmas Eve knowing both Santa and his reindeer were going to be satisfied when they visited our house.

6. **CHRISTMAS TALENT SHOW**
From Elyse

Every Christmas Eve, our parents host a family talent show. We've all come to expect performances that go above and beyond the traditional piano solo or vocal duet. In fact, some of us spend the whole year thinking about what we will perform! The person voted as being "most entertaining" gets to take home a traveling trophy to display for the next eleven months. We've seen everything from lip syncs to choreographed dances to magic tricks. Our children are now getting in on the act, too, making for even more friendly competition.

7. HOT CHOCOLATE BAR
From Elyse

Dad grew up going caroling with his family every Christmas season and has ensured that his tradition was passed down to our generation. Mom would put together plates of delicious treats for the neighbors, and we would bundle up and deliver them to all our friends while singing our favorite Christmas songs.

After being out in the cold and singing our little hearts out, we would come home and have a hot chocolate bar. Mom would make delicious hot chocolate and have an assortment of toppings we could pile on top. We loved drinking our yummy hot chocolate and warming up by the fire after a night of caroling!

8. A STOCKING FOR JESUS
From Camille

To help my kids learn what the Christmas season is all about, we sit down as a family and each write down one thing we want to give Jesus for Christmas. We don't give him "physical" gifts, but instead gifts of love and service (i.e., obey mom and dad, serve my sister by making her bed, clean up my room every day, play with my baby brother). We put the pieces of paper inside a special stocking that is just for Jesus, then hang the stocking on the mantel. On Christmas Day, after all the gifts have been opened, we take down the stocking for Jesus and talk about the gifts that we gave Him. It's a fun way to talk about how we served each other during the holidays and remember the true meaning of Christmas.

9. CHRISTMAS LISTS
From Lauren

One thing I remember most about Christmas when we younger was writing our Christmas lists. Most of the time we would start writing our Christmas list "drafts" in July, so by the time December came around, we were ready! Mom would set out paper and crayons or markers, and we would go to town! Mom has kept all of the lists from when we were younger and it is so fun to look back at all of thing we asked for. This is still one of my favorite traditions!

10. CHRISTMAS PAJAMAS
From Steph

One thing we all looked forward to every year was opening our Christmas pajamas. During the holiday season, we would go shopping with Mom and pick out a cute new pair of pajamas—and sometimes slippers to go with them! Mom would wrap them up and put them under the tree, with a special star on the To/From tag. As Christmas Eve drew to a close, we would gather around the tree and find our special starred packages and open them up, one

at a time. Then we'd all go put them on and have our picture taken together. We loved being able to open a present early, and it was so fun to have a new pair of pajamas to celebrate the holiday in!

11. OPENING CHRISTMAS STOCKINGS TOGETHER
From Steph

Every Christmas for as long as I can remember, we have opened our Christmas stockings together. We were always antsy on Christmas morning, but we would wait to go downstairs

and see what Santa had brought us until after we had opened our stockings. We would wake up and run into our parents' room and sit on their bed until Dad brought up an armful of stockings. It got squishy as we got older, but it was a tradition that brought us together every Christmas morning before the craziness of the day began. It was something I will never forget, and a tradition I will carry on with my children.

12. READING THE CHRISTMAS STORY
From Camille

When we were growing up, one of our favorite Christmas Eve traditions was to read the story of Christ's birth from the Bible and then act it out as a family. We would dress up in Mom and Dad's bathrobes, decide who would get the coveted role of Mary (with six girls, it was a battle every year), and act it out for our parents. It was the perfect way to end a fun day and remember the reason for the season.

Bacon and Egg Breakfast Casserole

This casserole is perfect for a holiday brunch!

3	cups croutons	1	green bell pepper, diced
¼	cup butter, melted	1	tablespoon prepared mustard
2	cups shredded cheddar cheese		Salt and pepper, to taste
6	eggs	12	slices bacon, cooked and crumbled
1¾	cups milk		

Preheat oven to 325 degrees F. Coat a 9x13-inch baking dish with nonstick cooking spray.

Spread croutons evenly in the prepared dish; drizzle with melted butter and then top with shredded cheddar cheese. In a medium bowl, whisk together eggs, milk, green pepper, mustard, salt, and pepper until combined. Pour egg mixture over cheese in baking dish and sprinkle with crumbled bacon. Bake 40 minutes. Allow casserole to stand 10 minutes before serving.

Makes 8 servings.

Homemade Orange Rolls

We can't imagine Christmas morning without these orange rolls. They are the perfect, sweet, gooey breakfast treat. To save time, make them the day before and warm them up before serving.

2 cups milk	½ teaspoon baking soda
½ cup vegetable oil	1½ teaspoons salt
1½ cups granulated sugar, divided	½ cup butter, softened
4½ cups all-purpose flour, divided	3 tablespoons orange juice
1 packet (2¼ teaspoons) active dry yeast	1 recipe Orange Glaze
½ teaspoon baking powder	

In a large saucepan over medium heat, combine milk, oil, and ½ cup of the sugar and heat until warm, but not scalding. (Temperature should read about 125 degrees F. on a candy thermometer.) Remove mixture from heat. Stir in 4 cups of the flour and the yeast. Cover pan with a tea towel or lid and let dough rest for 1 hour. Add the ½ cup remaining flour, baking powder, baking soda, and salt. Stir to combine.

Lightly flour a clean surface, and roll dough into a long, thin rectangle, approximately 12x18 inches.

Prepare filling in a small bowl, by combining remaining 1 cup sugar, softened butter, and orange juice. Spread filling evenly over the dough, making sure to reach all edges. Roll dough tightly, pinching the seam tightly once rolled. Slice dough into 24 pieces, using a serrated knife, pizza cutter, or unwaxed dental floss. (To ensure that your rolls are each the same size, first cut the rolled dough in half. Next, cut each half in half, so you have 4 pieces. Cut each of these pieces in half, to make 8 pieces. Cut each of the 8 pieces into 3.) Place rolls in a greased 9x13-inch baking pan. Cover and let rise 30 minutes.

Bake at 375 degrees F. for 20 to 25 minutes, or until golden brown. Cool just slightly before spreading Orange Glaze over the warm rolls.

Makes 24 rolls.

ORANGE GLAZE

2 cups powdered sugar	½ cup heavy cream
3 tablespoons orange juice	1 teaspoon orange extract

In a small bowl, beat together all ingredients until smooth and easily spreadable.

Baked Apple Pie French Toast

Another easy dish for Christmas morning, this recipe can be prepped the night before, refrigerated while Santa makes his deliveries, and then baked the next morning while you unwrap presents.

12 slices Texas toast	½ teaspoon ground nutmeg
1 (21-ounce) can apple pie filling	1 cup packed brown sugar
8 eggs	½ cup cold butter, cubed
2 cups milk	1 cup chopped pecans
2 teaspoons vanilla	2 tablespoons corn syrup
½ teaspoon ground cinnamon	

Arrange 6 slices of the bread in a greased 9x13-inch baking dish. Spread bread with pie filling and top with remaining bread slices. In a large bowl, whisk together the eggs, milk, vanilla, cinnamon, and nutmeg. Pour over bread. Cover and refrigerate overnight.

In the morning, remove from refrigerator 30 minutes before baking. Preheat oven to 350 degrees F.

Place brown sugar in a small bowl. Cut in butter until mixture resembles coarse crumbs. Stir in pecans and corn syrup. Sprinkle over French toast and bake, uncovered, 35 to 40 minutes, or until a knife inserted near the center comes out clean.

Makes 6 servings.

Gingerbread Waffles

Dad was the breakfast master at our house while we grew up. We always loved these Gingerbread Waffles—which are full of flavor and oh-so-festive—and we knew they had to make our list of Christmas brunch recipes.

1½ cups all-purpose flour	½ teaspoon salt
1½ teaspoons baking powder	2 eggs
½ teaspoon baking soda	⅓ cup granulated sugar
1 teaspoon ground cinnamon	¾ cup milk
¾ teaspoon ground ginger	½ cup molasses
¼ teaspoon ground nutmeg	¼ cup butter, melted
Pinch ground cloves	

Preheat waffle iron.

In a large bowl, combine flour, baking powder, baking soda, cinnamon, ginger, nutmeg, cloves, and salt.

In a separate bowl, beat the eggs and sugar together until thick and foamy. Stir in the milk and molasses. Add liquid mixture to the dry ingredients and stir until well-combined. Slowly fold in the melted butter.

Spray hot waffle iron with nonstick cooking spray. Follow the manufacturer's directions for your waffle maker to measure batter and cook waffles until finished.

Top waffles with powdered sugar, whipped cream and fresh fruit, or your favorite syrup.

The number of servings varies depending on the size of the waffle iron.

Warm Spiced Cider

Visiting Grandma on Christmas Day was a family tradition. Her amazing cooking always made her house smell delicious. On Christmas morning she would whip up a pot of this spiced cider and let it simmer all day long. Just one whiff of it these days brings back many happy memories!

1	gallon apple cider	1	teaspoon whole cloves
½	cup brown sugar	3	whole cinnamon sticks
¼	teaspoon salt	¼	teaspoon ground nutmeg
1	teaspoon ground allspice		

In a large stockpot or slow cooker, bring cider to a simmer over medium heat.

Place brown sugar, salt, and spices on a six-inch square of clean cheesecloth or any clean, thin cotton fabric. Pull up edges and tie with a string to form a bag. Reduce heat under the cider to maintain a low simmer. Place bag in cider and continue to simmer at least 20 minutes or for several hours.

If using a slow cooker, heat cider and spices on low 2 to 3 hours, and then keep warm. Refrigerate leftovers and reheat as needed.

Makes about 16 (1-cup) servings.

Nutella Banana Bread

This banana bread is incredibly moist and has the perfect amount of Nutella in it. Be sure to double the recipe because the bread will be eaten quickly!

2 cups all-purpose flour	2 large eggs
¾ teaspoon baking soda	1¼ cups mashed ripe bananas
½ teaspoon salt	⅓ cup milk
¼ cup unsalted butter, at room temperature	1 teaspoon vanilla
1 cup granulated sugar	¾ heaping cup Nutella

Preheat oven to 350 degrees F. Coat an 8x4-inch loaf pan with nonstick cooking spray.

In a medium bowl, whisk together flour, baking soda, and salt.

In a separate large bowl, beat butter and sugar with an electric mixer at medium speed until blended. Add eggs one at a time, beating well after each addition. Add banana, milk, and vanilla and mix until blended.

Slowly add flour mixture to wet ingredients, mixing just until incorporated. Do not over mix.

Spoon Nutella into a small, microwave-safe bowl and soften in the microwave 15 seconds on high power. Add 1 cup of the banana bread batter to the Nutella and stir until blended well. Alternately spoon batter mixed with Nutella and plain batter into the prepared pan. Use a knife to swirl batters together.

Bake 50 to 60 minutes. (A toothpick inserted in the center should come out clean.) The bread will seem a tiny bit undercooked due to the texture of the Nutella. Cool 15 minutes in the pan, then turn out onto a wire rack to cool completely.

Gooey Caramel Pull-Aparts

There's nothing like the smell of delicious caramel pull-apart bread baking on Christmas morning. Mom often made this in just minutes on Christmas Eve after we had all gone to bed, and then she stuck it in the oven first thing Christmas morning for a stress-free, gooey treat. If you don't own a Bundt pan, try using two loaf pans.

16 frozen dinner rolls, such as Rhodes	½ cup chopped pecans or walnuts
1 (3.5-ounce) package cook-and-serve butterscotch pudding (not instant)	¾ cup brown sugar
	6 tablespoons butter, melted

Thaw frozen rolls in a zipper-top bag for approximately 2 hours. They should be just barely thawed, with no rising time.

Use kitchen shears or clean scissors to cut each roll into 6 pieces. Coat a Bundt pan with nonstick cooking spray. Sprinkle all of the nuts into the pan. Arrange half of the cut rolls atop the nuts. Sprinkle half a package of dry pudding mix over rolls. In a small bowl, mix together sugar and melted butter. Drizzle half of the butter-sugar mixture over rolls. Top with remaining cut rolls, pudding mix, and sugar-butter mixture. Cover with plastic wrap coated with nonstick cooking spray and let rise overnight, or at least 8 hours.

Bake at 350 degrees F. for 30 to 35 minutes. Cool no longer than 5 minutes. Turn pan over on serving dish and enjoy!

Makes 10 servings.

Homemade French Toast Sticks

Warm breakfast foods in the winter are one of our favorite things. Mom used to buy us French Toast Sticks for breakfast during Christmas break, and it was always such a treat! These Homemade French Toast Sticks bring back those good memories but taste so much better than the ones from a box.

8 slices white Texas Toast bread	1 tablespoon granulated sugar
5 eggs	2 teaspoons ground cinnamon
1 cup heavy cream	3 tablespoons butter
2 tablespoons milk	Powdered sugar, for topping
1 tablespoon vanilla	Maple syrup, for topping

Cut each slice of bread into 4 equal strips and set aside. In a large bowl, whisk together eggs, cream, milk, vanilla, sugar, and cinnamon. Melt butter in a large skillet over medium heat. Once butter is melted, dip each piece of bread in egg mixture, let excess drip off, and then place in skillet. If skillet is on the small side, do this in batches so the sticks are not overcrowded. Once one side is golden brown, flip sticks and cook until both sides are golden brown and crispy on the outside. Sprinkle with powdered sugar and serve with maple syrup.

Makes 6 servings.

Cherry Chocolate Muffins

Christmas is not complete without a delicious treat that combines cherries and chocolate! These muffins bring the great flavor combo straight to your breakfast table. They are easy to put together sure to please all of your guests.

1	(15.25-ounce) box chocolate cake mix	⅓	cup vegetable oil
1	teaspoon baking powder	3	large eggs
2	tablespoons all-purpose flour	1	cup chocolate chips
⅔	cup milk	1 to 2	cups fresh (or frozen) dark sweet cherries, pitted and chopped

Preheat oven to 375 degrees F. Line 18 muffin tins with paper cupcake liners; set aside.

In a large bowl, stir together dry cake mix, baking powder, flour, milk, oil, and eggs until well combined. Fold in cherries and chocolate chips, reserving a few cherries and a few chocolate chips to sprinkle on top. Spoon batter into prepared muffin cups, filling about two-thirds full. Sprinkle reserved cherries and chocolate chips on top. Bake 15 to 20 minutes, until a toothpick inserted in center comes out clean.

Makes about 18 muffins.

Eggs a la Goldenrod

You can't go wrong with this delicious, golden gravy with hard-boiled eggs over toast.

◇◇◇

½ cup butter	Salt and pepper, to taste
½ cup all-purpose flour	8 hard-boiled eggs, peeled
4 cups milk	8 slices white bread, toasted

Melt butter in a large saucepan over medium heat. Whisk in flour and cook 10 minutes, stirring often, to make a golden-brown roux. Gradually pour in the milk and bring to a simmer, whisking constantly. Reduce heat to low and cook 10 more minutes, whisking occasionally. Season with salt and pepper to taste.

Separate hard-boiled egg yolks from whites. Chop the egg whites and stir into the gravy. Crumble the yolks with a fork and set aside.

To serve, place toasted bread on a plate, cover with gravy, and garnish with egg yolk.

Makes 8 servings.

Brunch Enchiladas

If you love omelets and enchiladas, then this recipe will become a holiday favorite. It's a loaded enchilada cooked in beaten eggs and is perfect for a holiday brunch.

½ cup chopped fresh mushrooms	8 flour tortillas
½ cup chopped green onions	2 cups shredded cheddar cheese, divided
1 red pepper, chopped	1 cup milk
1 green pepper, chopped	6 eggs, lightly beaten
2 cups cubed cooked ham	¼ teaspoon salt (optional)

In a large, nonstick skillet over medium-high heat, cook mushrooms, onions, and peppers until peppers are soft. Stirring often so the peppers don't stick to the bottom of the pan.

Stir in ham cubes and cook until heated through. Remove from heat. Spoon ¼ cup of the ham-and-vegetable mixture down the center of each tortilla. Top each with 2 tablespoons shredded cheese. Roll up tortillas and place seam-side down in a greased 9x13-inch baking dish.

In a large bowl, combine the milk, eggs, and salt, if using, whisking until smooth. Pour over tortillas. Cover with foil and refrigerate 8 hours or overnight.

Remove enchiladas from the refrigerator 30 minutes before baking. Preheat oven to 350 degrees F. Bake, covered, 25 minutes. Uncover and bake an additional 10 minutes. Sprinkle with remaining cheese and continue baking just until cheese is melted. Let stand 10 minutes before serving.

Makes 8 servings.

Homemade Waffles with Chocolate-Hazelnut Sauce

These waffles are a breeze to make and taste much better than any mix.

2 cups all-purpose flour	1½ cups milk
1 teaspoon salt	⅓ cup butter, melted
4 teaspoons baking powder	1 teaspoon vanilla
2 tablespoons granulated sugar	Strawberries, for topping
2 eggs	Whipped cream, for topping

CHOCOLATE-HAZELNUT SAUCE

1 cup chocolate syrup	½ cup chocolate hazelnut spread, such as Nutella

Preheat waffle iron.

In a large mixing bowl, combine flour, salt, baking powder, and sugar. In a separate bowl, beat the eggs and then stir in milk, butter, and vanilla. Pour liquid mixture into flour mixture and stir until just combined. Follow the manufacturer's directions for your waffle maker to measure batter and cook waffles until golden brown and crispy.

In a small saucepan over low heat, whisk together chocolate syrup and hazelnut spread until warmed through. Serve over waffles. Top with strawberries and whipped cream.

The number of servings varies, depending on the size of the waffle iron.

12

SANITY-SAVING

CHRISTMAS TIPS

The holidays can be so crazy. Between the parties, programs, and presents and all the other activities associated with the holidays, it can be exhausting! These are 12 ways that have helped us cut back on the craziness during the season so we can focus on the true spirit of Christmas.

1. **Keep Your Christmas Decorations Organized.** We have found that it's much easier to get excited about decorating if your lights, ornaments, and other decorations are carefully organized. Your type of organization can be as simple as keeping your lights in one box, your tree decorations in one box, and your family room decorations and kitchen decorations in another box. Here are a few additional tips:

    • Number storage boxes in the order you would like to bring them out and decorate.

    • Label the outside of each storage box with a broad description, such as "tree ornaments." Inside each box, include a master list of the box's contents.

    • Use old belts to cinch artificial Christmas trees and thus save space.

    • Keep gift wrap and wrapping supplies in a separate container that can be easily accessed throughout the season rather than stored in the garage or attic until it's time to repack.

    • Keep ornaments from breaking by packing them with old newspapers in recycled fruit containers. (The apple and orange containers work best. You can often get them from the grocery store. And best of all: they stack!)

    • Keep wire hooks and smaller ornaments in separate boxes so the wires won't scratch the ornaments.

    • Wrap your Christmas lights around empty wrapping paper tubes to save yourself from the dreaded tangle of lights.

2. **Decorate as a Family.** An extra pair of hands during the holidays is invaluable. Make it a tradition to set up the Christmas decorations together as a family. As your children get older, they can even be responsible for a specific area or item.

3. **Make and Keep a Budget.** Save yourself stress by setting a budget early on—maybe as early as July—and sticking to it. Write down each purchase for each family member as soon as it is made. Save receipts. Stop spending when your limit is reached. Don't forget to add up how much all those little items, such as stocking stuffers, cost.

4. **Shop Smart.** Making a list is the first step to shopping smart. Remind yourself to stick to the list and not buy something just because it is available on a blow-out sale or Black Friday event. Throughout the year, keep track of prices on items you are likely to purchase as gifts (Lego sets, dolls, kitchen appliances, books, etc.). This will help you decide whether or not those Black Friday or Cyber Monday deals really are amazing.

5. **Wrap Well.** Let each child choose a favorite color or pattern of wrapping paper and use that to wrap his or her presents. Your kids will love being able to see which presents are just for them under the tree. This will also make the unwrapping process on Christmas morning much easier.

6. **Meal Plan.** Sometimes during the hustle and bustle of the holiday season, it's much easier to just buy a pizza and let the kids take care of themselves! But don't forget the importance of spending time together as a family, especially this time of year. Planning out a weekly menu in advance will save you time and stress because you will already know what's for dinner. Memories will be made throughout the whole season as you sit down and eat together.

7. **Use Your Slow Cooker.** Need to make dinner on Christmas day? Your slow cooker can be your best friend. Use it to make just about anything, saving you loads of time and work in the kitchen. Try out the following recipes to get you started:

- Slow-Cooker Ham with Honey Mustard Glaze, page 99
- Slow-Cooker Ham and Pineapple Sandwiches, page 100
- Slow-Cooker Balsamic Pot Roast, page 103
- Slow-Cooker Chicken and Gravy, page 104
- Slow-Cooker Chicken Fajita Soup, page 107
- Slow-Cooker Texas Chili, page 109

8. **Don't Procrastinate.** Don't try and tackle it all in one day or wait until December 23 to finally start making gifts for your coworkers and neighbors. The last thing you need that close to Christmas is an entire day in the kitchen. Plan ahead, and stick with the plan. You will be able to enjoy your holiday season stress free!

9. **Digital Christmas Cards.** As times change, the etiquette for Christmas correspondence has changed as well, allowing for digitally created and sent Christmas cards. Not only do email cards cost less and take less time to produce, they are also a greener way to send holiday wishes. There are hundreds of cute templates and online scrapbook paper you can use for free. And a digital copy of your card can be saved and accessed throughout the year.

    If you prefer to send more personal, hand-written Christmas greetings, start early in the season, gathering friends' addresses through-out the year and writing a few cards a day beginning in November.

10. **Offer Service Instead of Gifts.** Gather your neighbors, co-workers, extended family, or church group and consider agreeing to forego gifts this year. Instead, meet together to perform a service project or hold a fun activity. One community we know of invited all the children in the neighborhood to come out and go sledding.

The adults made and passed out hot chocolate, while also collecting money to be donated to a local food bank. (For a delicious twist on an old favorite, try the frozen hot chocolate recipe below.)

Other ideas include serving together at a local soup kitchen, visiting and donating to a homeless shelter, organizing a Sub-for-Santa project, and Christmas caroling at a senior center or the homes of widows in your neighborhood.

FROZEN HOT CHOCOLATE

1   cup hot cocoa powder

3   tablespoons sugar

3   cups milk

6   cups ice

    Whipped topping, for garnish

    Chocolate syrup, for garnish

    Chocolate shavings, for garnish

Add the cocoa powder, sugar, milk, and ice to a blender and blend until smooth. Pour into glasses and top with whipped topping, a drizzle of chocolate syrup, and chocolate shavings.

Makes 10 servings.

11. **Give Family Gifts.** With six grown sisters, our family grows a little (and sometimes a lot) each year. To make shopping easier, we have started giving family gifts instead of individual gifts. Each family puts their name in a bowl, and each family draws out another name. Coming up with family gifts is always so much fun. We usually set the budget pretty low and all agree to stick to it. Some great family gift ideas include:

- A family movie and treat bucket
- A family picnic basket filled with fun picnic foods, a blanket, and maybe a simple outdoor game
- A puzzle
- A family membership to the local zoo or waterpark
- A donation to charity in the family's name, with an ornament as a memento
- A board game

- A coupon for an evening of babysitting so the parents can go out on a date
- A family "arts and crafts" basket with paper, glue, clay, markers, etc.
- Tickets to a local sporting event
- A Netflix or Hulu subscription
- An ice cream maker
- Prepay for a family photo session

12. **Remember That It Doesn't Have to Be Perfect.** Remind yourself—daily if needed—that everyone is going to be happy, everyone is going to have fun, and nobody is going to remember the tiny details that worried you for days. Concentrate on your family and make lasting memories. In the end that's all that is going to be remembered.

12

CHRISTMAS PARTY IDEAS

Some of our fondest Christmas memories are of holiday parties. We loved being with our cousins and playing games. Food was a big part of our celebrations, and spending quality time with those we love was—and still is—priceless. Our parents continue to host an annual Christmas party where we play some of the same party games—and devour some of the same refreshments—that made Christmas magical so many years ago.

1. **Candy Sled Race.** This game is great fun for all ages. Over the years we have experimented with all kinds of makeshift racetracks. Sometimes it was a folding banquet table, laid flat with one end propped on the back of a couch to create a nice slope. Other years we have used an 8-foot piece of wood. Be creative and use whatever you have around the house.

   - Brown paper bags
   - Candy canes
   - Craft sticks
   - Chocolate Santas
   - Original Snickers bars
   - Snickers Fun Size bars
   - 1 roll Scotch tape per team
   - Miscellaneous Christmas candy
   - Bowl
   - Timer

Before the party, fill 1 brown paper bag for each team. In each bag, place 2 candy canes, 2 craft sticks, 1 chocolate Santa, 1 original Snickers Bar, 1 Snickers Fun Size bar, and 1 roll Scotch tape.

When ready to play, divide into teams of 3 to 4 people. Put miscellaneous Christmas candy in a bowl and have each team pick out a predetermined number of candies. Give each team 1 filled paper bag.

Set the timer for 10 minutes. At the start signal, each team can begin building a candy sled, using everything in the bag, plus all of the candy selected from the bowl.

When the timer goes off, each team must stop building.

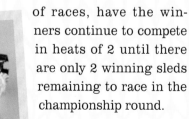

Put up your track and race the sleds against each other in heats of 2. After the first round of races, have the winners continue to compete in heats of 2 until there are only 2 winning sleds remaining to race in the championship round.

2. **Toast the Season.** Family Christmas parties were never complete without this drink. Grandma made it every year, and we could never get enough.

FRAPPÉ

1 carton vanilla ice cream, slightly softened

1 carton raspberry sherbet, slightly softened

1 (2-liter) bottle lemon-lime soda

Scoop the ice cream and sherbet into a large punch bowl. Slowly pour in the soda and stir gently. Let mixture sit 5 minutes to melt just a bit. Stir again to blend the ice creams together. There will be some ice cream chunks in the drink—which is partly why it's so delicious.

3. **Santa's Helper.** This game is so hilarious! Each team starts with the same supplies, but no two Santas ever look alike at the end. Mix kids and grownups together in teams so no one team has the advantage. Feel free to add other items to the supply list to make your Santas more unique.

- Red tissue paper (or crepe paper)
- Masking tape
- White batting
- Black construction paper
- Kid scissors
- Timer

Divide into teams of 3 to 4 people and give each team the following: 6 to 7 sheets red tissue paper, 1 roll masking tape, 1 big chunk white batting, 1 sheet black construction paper, and 1 pair scissors. Set a timer for 10 to 15 minutes. Each team has until the timer goes off to turn a team member into Santa.

4. **Christmas Caroling in a Flatbed Trailer.** A caroling party with friends or family can be super fun and super easy to throw together. Hitch a flatbed trailer to a pickup truck, load everyone on, and ride slowly through the neighborhood singing Christmas carols.

Stop at selected homes to knock and sing, but don't stop singing while the trailer is moving. Your carols will be heard up and down the street. When finished, head back to a central location for hot chocolate and a simple treat, such as our Double-Decker Fudge on page 71.

5. **White Elephant Gift Exchange.** This gift exchange was one of our favorite party games growing up. To mix it up from year to year, consider giving the exchange a theme. Some ideas include Hollywood, books, transportation, purple, summer, nature, and so on. Be creative and make sure everyone agrees to a price limit. Let people know they can purchase the item or find something around the house to re-gift. Be sure to announce the Gift Exchange in advance and remind people several times so no one shows up without a wrapped gift. And be prepared: this game can get intense as guests plot (and steal!) to get the gift they want most.

  • Small slips of paper
  • Pencils
  • Basket or bowl

When guests arrive, have them place their gifts in a pile in the middle of the floor. On a slip of paper, write a number for each person attending the party. Place the papers in a bowl or basket.

To play: Each guest draws a slip of a paper to determine the order they will pick a gift from the pile. The person who picks number 1 goes first. He or she picks any gift from the pile, opens it, and shows everyone what it is. The next person can either take a gift that has already been opened or choose an unwrapped gift from the pile. When a gift is stolen, the person stolen from picks an unwrapped gift from the pile and opens it. Once a gift has been stolen 3 times, it is safe and cannot be taken anymore. The person with the highest number picks last and can choose any gift he or she wants. After the final gift is opened, the game ends.

6. **Christmas Piñata.** Piñatas at Christmas parties were a tradition in both Mom and Dad's families growing up. Naturally, that means a piñata will forever be a part of our parties. We don't always have a Christmas-themed piñata. Sometimes we pick a theme to go along with a movie or book. Recently we made a Minion piñata (from the *Despicable Me* movie franchise) described below. The kids loved it! If you make your own piñata, start several days in advance to allow it to dry and harden properly.

  • 2 (9-inch) balloons
  • 10 small balloons, such as water bomb balloons

- Duct tape
- 12 wooden skewers
- Newspaper cut into 2x8-inch strips
- Flour
- Water
- White crepe paper, cut into 2-inch squares
- Blue crepe paper, cut into 2-inch squares
- Yellow crepe paper, cut into 2-inch squares
- Scissors
- 4 ounces Elmer's glue
- 1 paper plate
- Pencil with an eraser
- Sharpie
- Cardboard or poster board for arms
- 1 piece black cardstock or construction paper for hands and feet
- Hot glue gun with glue stick
- 6 feet heavy twine or string
- Candy, for filling the piñata

❋ Blow up the balloons. Tape the knotted ends of the 2 larger balloons together.

❋ Have someone hold the 2 balloons so that a 3- to 4-inch gap remains between them. With duct tape, attach 12 skewers evenly around the top balloon. Tape the ends of the skewers to the bottom balloon.

❋ Fill in the gaps between the large balloons with the smaller balloons. If needed, stuff some crumpled newspaper around the small balloons to finish making the shape of a minion and to fill all gaps.

❋ In a large bowl or casserole dish, mix equal parts flour and water (1 cup flour to 1 cup water is a good place to start).

❋ Balance the bottom balloon in a mixing bowl so it stands on its own.

❋ Dip a newspaper strip in the flour-water mixture. Gently wipe off the excess batter and lay the strip of paper over the top balloon. Continue this process to cover all but a 3-inch opening at the top of the balloon (where you'll put the candy in).

❋ Let the piñata dry 6 hours or overnight. Once dry, flip over the piñata, make another batch of the flour-water mixture, dip the newspaper strips in the mixture, and layer over the rest of the balloons. Let dry 6 hours or overnight.

❋ Cover piñata with two additional layers.

❋ When layers are hard and dry, pop the balloons and then pull out the sticks, popped balloons, and crunched up newspaper.

* With a Sharpie, draw the Minion's face and overalls on the piñata shell.

* Squirt a dollop of Elmer's glue onto a paper plate. Twist a square of crepe paper around the eraser end of a pencil, dip the end in glue, and stick it on the piñata. To make it easier to see where each color goes, glue a twisted piece of crepe paper inside each area as a sort of color code.

* Repeat until Minion is completely covered.

* Draw the arms freehand-style on a piece of cardboard and cut them out. Draw the feet and hands on the black cardstock or construction paper and cut them out.

* Wrap the arms in blue crepe paper, using hot glue to secure them. Glue hands to arms. Glue feet to the bottom of the piñata and arms to the sides.

* Punch a hole on each side of the opening at the top of the piñata. Thread the twine or string through the holes. Bring the ends up and tie in a square knot so you can hang it on a broomstick or from the ceiling.

* Fill the piñata with candy.

7. **Ugly Sweater Contest.** Need another activity at your party? Have an ugly sweater contest. Be sure to include a note on the invitation about the contest and encourage guests to wear the ugliest holiday sweaters they can find! Holiday sweaters can easily be found at thrift stores, or perhaps in the back of your parents' closet! During the party, guests can view one another's sweaters and then vote for the ugliest one.

Here are some ideas you can try to make your Christmas sweater uglier:

• Attach a string of lights, complete with a battery pack

• Glue on a bird's nest

• Glue on a small wrapped box or two

• Make snowmen with white pom-poms and glue them on

• Glue on ornaments, tinsel, or garland

• Glue on bows or Christmas buttons

• Trim sleeves and collar with tinsel or red faux fur

8. **Indoor Snowball Fight.** Who wouldn't love a good indoor snowball fight with all of the cousins? You can buy packages of stuffed white fabric balls that look like snowballs or easily make your own.

- Small Styrofoam balls
- Cotton balls or white pom-poms
- Glue

Glue cotton balls all around a small Styrofoam ball, making several layers. Let the glue dry before having the kids go at it. The balls are so soft that no one should get hurt, although you may want to play it safe and put away anything valuable during the snowball fight.

9. **Cookie Exchange.** A Cookie Exchange can be part of a larger party or the party itself. When sending invites, ask everyone to bring 1 to 2 dozen cookies, along with 1 to 2 dozen copies of the recipe (amount can be more or less depending on your invite list). Decorate a table with a nice Christmas tablecloth and leave place cards out for guests to write their names and the type of cookie they've brought. Guests can place the cookies, recipes, and place cards around the table to share with the crowd. These Red Velvet Cream Cheese cookies and White Macadamia Nut cookies are perfect for a Cookie Exchange.

RED VELVET CREAM CHEESE COOKIES

- ½ cup butter, softened
- 1 (8-ounce) cream cheese, softened
- 1 large egg
- 1 teaspoon vanilla
- 1 (15.25-ounce) box red velvet cake mix
- ½ cup white chocolate chips
- ½ cup powdered sugar

Preheat oven to 350 degrees F.

In a large bowl, combine butter and cream cheese using an electric mixer, until fluffy.

Add egg and vanilla. Mix until completely incorporated, then add cake mix and continue mixing until a thick dough forms. Fold in chocolate chips.

Place powdered sugar in a small bowl.

Using a cookie scoop, form one-inch dough balls and roll in powdered sugar to coat.

Place cookies 2 inches apart on a parchment-lined cookie sheet and bake for 10 to 12 minutes until centers are set.

Cool on wire rack.

When completely cooled, dust cookies with powdered sugar.

Makes about 30 cookies.

WHITE CHOCOLATE MACADAMIA NUT COOKIES

1 cup margarine, softened

1 cup brown sugar

½ cup sugar

2 eggs, beaten

1 teaspoon vanilla

3 cups flour

1 teaspoon baking powder

1 teaspoon baking soda

¼ teaspoon salt

1½ cups white chocolate chips

1½ cups macadamia nuts, coarsely chopped

Preheat oven to 350 degrees F.

Cream maragarine and sugars. Add beaten eggs and vanilla.

Stir in flour, baking powder, baking soda, and salt. Mix well.

Add white chocolate chips and macadamia nuts.

Chill dough for about 30 minutes. Roll into 1½-inch balls.

Bake on ungreased cookie sheet for 8 to 10 minutes. Do not overbake.

Makes 3 dozen cookies.

10. **Progressive Dinner.** Progressive dinners involve some planning ahead but are a great way to get to know several families in your neighborhood and enjoy a holiday meal together.

It's best to include 3 or 4 families who all live in the same neighborhood or area of the city. Each family is assigned a course, such as appetizers, soup and/or salad, main dish, and dessert.

Everyone meets at the first house for the appetizer and then caravans to each subsequent house for the remaining courses. You may choose to have each family share something (a talent, a favorite Christmas tradition, a round of caroling) at their own home or simply let everyone visit and enjoy the company at each stop.

You could also set a theme for the meal, such as comfort food, Italian food, sweet and savory, Mexican food, and so on.

11. **Play-Doh Pictionary.** This fun game can include all the little kids in the family and doesn't take much more than a bunch of words on cards and a couple cans of Play-Doh.

- 2 cans Play-Doh
- Index cards with 1 word or phrase from the following list on each card
- 2-minute timer

Before playing, write one of the words or phrase below on each index card (if some of your players are too young to read, find an image and glue it next to each word):

- Angel
- Baby Jesus
- Boot
- Bow
- Candle
- Candy cane
- Chimney
- Christmas tree
- Mitten
- Ornament
- Present
- Rudolph
- Santa
- Scarf
- Sleigh
- Snowflake
- Snowman
- Star
- Stocking

To play, divide into 2 teams. Give each team a can of Play-Doh. Have 1 team pick a player to go first.

That player picks an index card, flips it over, and reads the word or looks at the picture without letting the other teammates know what it is. The player then molds the Play-Doh while teammates shout out guesses. The other team keeps time while this is happening and shouts, "Time's up" at the 2-minute mark.

If no one on the team guesses the correct answer, the other team gets a chance to try. Take turns going back and forth between teams, awarding 1 point for each correct guess.

12. **Relay Race.** We love relay races! Sometimes we play in 2 teams; other times we play individually and each person goes through each relay station. If playing in teams, the first team to finish the last station wins. If playing individually, each person is timed as he or she completes the relay. The person with the shortest time wins. We've found that setting up 5 stations works best. Be creative as you think of ideas for each station, and try using things you already have on hand. Here are some ideas for stations to set up throughout the house, the family room, or (if you're lucky enough to live in a mild climate) the backyard:

- Eat a donut hanging from a string; no hands allowed.

- Hit a golf ball across the room with a carrot attached to a string. The string is tied to your belt loop. Put a piece of masking tape on the carpet as the starting line and another one as the finish line. Each player/team must cross the finish line in order to move to the next station.

- With mittens or heavy snow gloves on, unwrap a piece of Dubble Bubble gum, chew it, and blow a bubble.

- Blow up a balloon, tie it, and then sit on it until it pops.

- Toss a handful of bean bags into an ice cream bucket across the room.

Gingerbread Cookie Bars

These gingerbread cookie bars drastically simplify the cookie-making process. Instead of rolling out dough and cutting out dozens of gingerbread men, you get all the delicious gingerbread flavor in an easy-to-make cookie bar. They are chewy and soft and packed with holiday flavor. Plus, they are easy enough that your kids can help you make them!

½ cup butter, melted

¾ cup granulated sugar

¼ cup brown sugar

½ teaspoon vanilla

⅓ cup molasses

1 egg

2 teaspoons baking soda

2 cups all-purpose flour

1 tablespoon ground cinnamon

½ teaspoon ground ginger

¼ teaspoon ground cloves

¼ teaspoon ground nutmeg

½ teaspoon salt

1 recipe of your favorite cream cheese frosting (optional)

Powdered sugar, for dusting (optional)

Preheat oven to 350 degrees F. Coat a 9x13-inch baking dish with nonstick cooking spray and set aside.

In a large bowl, beat butter, sugar, brown sugar, vanilla, and molasses on medium speed until creamy. Add the egg and stir until completely incorporated. Add flour, spices, and salt and mix until well combined. Spread dough into prepared pan, using clean hands or a rubber spatula to press the dough to the edges of the pan. Bake 15 to 20 minutes; bars should be a little moist. Cool in the pan on a wire rack.

When cooled, frost with cream cheese frosting or dust lightly with powdered sugar, if desired. Or, don't top them with anything. They are delicious no matter what you do! Cut into squares and serve.

Makes 24 bars.

Peanut Butter Snowballs

These little snowballs are easy to make and are always a big hit. For the white chocolate coating, try using Wilton Candy Melts or Guittard White Chocolate Wafers. Almond bark also works well.

1   cup powdered sugar

½   cup creamy peanut butter

3   tablespoons butter, softened

1   pound white candy melts or almond bark

Silver sugar sprinkles (optional)

Line a large baking sheet with parchment or waxed paper and set aside.

In a medium bowl, combine sugar, peanut butter, and butter until mixed well. Shape dough into 1-inch balls and place on prepared baking sheet. Move dough balls to the refrigerator to set until firm. Don't let the dough get too cold. Cold dough is prone to expanding when covered in hot melting candy and can lead to cracks in the candy as it hardens.

In another medium-sized bowl, melt candy coating according to package directions. Dip balls gently in the candy coating, using a two-pronged fork to move the balls around and then lift them out. Place balls on prepared baking sheet. If desired, immediately sprinkle the tops with sprinkles. Refrigerate until chilled.

Makes 24 to 30 snowballs.

Double-Decker Fudge

Our mom was notorious for making Christmas goodie plates for friends and neighbors. She would spend a couple of days in the kitchen baking up a storm; and it was torture as a child to smell all those yummy cookies and treats and know that they were going to be given away. One of our favorite treats was her Double-Decker Fudge—the perfect combination of chocolate and peanut butter. If you don't need to make fudge to feed the masses, you can easily cut this recipe in half and use an 8x8-inch baking pan.

1   (12-ounce) bag peanut butter chips

1   (12-ounce) bag semisweet chocolate chips

4½ cups granulated sugar

2   (7-ounce) jars marshmallow crème

1½ cups evaporated milk

½   cup butter

2   teaspoons vanilla

Line a 9x13-inch baking pan with aluminum foil and set aside.

Pour peanut butter chips into 1 large bowl and chocolate chips into a second large bowl; set aside.

In a large saucepan over medium heat, combine the sugar, marshmallow crème, evaporated milk, and butter. Cook and stir until mixture comes to a boil, and then stir continuously for 5 minutes (let it boil the entire time you are stirring). Remove saucepan from heat and add vanilla.

Carefully pour half of the mixture over the peanut butter chips and the other half over the chocolate chips. Stir the peanut butter chips until they are melted and the mixture is smooth, about 2 minutes. Pour the peanut butter mixture into the bottom of the foil-lined pan.

Stir the chocolate chip mixture until the chips are completely melted and the mixture is smooth. Slowly and carefully pour this mixture over the peanut butter layer in the pan. Use a rubber spatula to gently spread the chocolate mixture to the edges of the pan.

Let the fudge cool 5 minutes before placing in the refrigerator. Allow fudge to set up and chill 2 to 4 hours. Cut and serve.

Store in an airtight container at room temperature. Fudge will also last 3 to 5 days in the refrigerator and 3 months in the freezer.

Makes 48 to 60 servings, depending on how large or small you cut the pieces.

Pumpkin Pie Cake

A cross between pumpkin pie and cake, this dish is pumpkin-y, moist, and so delicious! Serve on its own or topped with whipped cream or vanilla ice cream.

1 (15-ounce) can pure pumpkin	1 teaspoon ground cinnamon
1 (12-ounce) can evaporated milk	1 teaspoon pumpkin pie spice
1½ cups granulated sugar	1 yellow cake mix
3 eggs, beaten	1 cup butter, melted
½ teaspoon salt	1 cup chopped pecans or walnuts

Preheat oven to 350 degrees F. Grease a 9x13-inch baking dish and set aside.

In a large bowl mix together the pumpkin, evaporated milk, sugar, eggs, salt, cinnamon, and pumpkin pie spice. Pour into prepared pan. Sprinkle dry cake mix evenly over the entire pumpkin mixture. Be sure to use all of the cake mix. Pour melted butter evenly over the top of the cake mix. Top with chopped nuts. Bake 55 minutes, until the top begins to brown and set. Serve warm or cold.

Makes about 20 servings.

Almond English Toffee

When trays of Christmas treats are spread out, it's the English toffee that's always first to disappear! This is the perfect toffee for giving or just indulging in for your own pleasure! It's easy to make and doesn't require a candy thermometer.

1½ cups whole, unblanched almonds	¼ teaspoon salt
1 cup salted butter	½ tablespoon hot water
1 cup granulated sugar	1 (12-ounce) bag milk chocolate chips
½ teaspoon vanilla	½ cup finely chopped pecans

Line a 9x13-inch baking pan with aluminum foil and set aside.

Spread a single layer of the almonds on a microwave-safe plate. Cook on high power in 1-minute increments until the nuts are crisp and fragrant. You may need to do this in batches so the almonds remain in a single layer.

Arrange toasted almonds in a single layer on the prepared baking sheet.

In a heavy, 2-quart saucepan, cook the butter, sugar, vanilla, and salt over medium-high heat, stirring constantly with a wooden spoon. Just when the butter mixture is all melted, pour in ½ tablespoon hot water. (Be sure to add this before the mixture really starts to cook.) Continue to stir constantly 7 to 9 minutes, or until color starts to brown. (It may even start to smoke lightly at the end of the cooking time.) Immediately pour the hot butter mixture over the almonds in the foil-lined pan. The toffee sets up fast, so pour quickly. Sprinkle the chocolate chips over the hot mixture. Let the chocolate chips sit for about 1 minute so they begin to melt. Using a butter knife or spatula, spread the melted chocolate over the toffee. Sprinkle with chopped pecans. Pat the pecans very gently into the chocolate with your hands. Let toffee cool 1 hour to allow the chocolate to set up. Break into pieces and party!

Store for up to 2 weeks in an airtight container.

Makes approximately 30 servings.

Eggnog Gingerbread Trifle

If you love the holiday flavors of eggnog and gingerbread, you'll polish off this trifle in minutes. If you'd rather use a favorite recipe for gingerbread or purchase it at a bakery, omit the first three ingredients.

1 (14.5-ounce) box spice cake mix	3 cups eggnog
1 tablespoon molasses	2 cups non-dairy whipped topping, or 2 cups sweetened whipped cream
1 teaspoon ground nutmeg	¼ cup dried cranberries
1 (5.1-ounce) package instant vanilla pudding	8 to 10 gingersnap cookies

Prepare cake mix according to package directions, adding the 1 tablespoon molasses and 1 teaspoon ground nutmeg with the ingredients called for on the box. Bake cake as directed, using any size pan. Let it cool completely.

Pour the pudding mix in a large bowl and whisk in eggnog until it is completely incorporated, about 2 minutes. Refrigerate until ready to assemble the trifle.

Crumble half of the cooled cake into the bottom of a large glass bowl or trifle dish. Cover with half of the pudding mixture, followed by 1 cup whipped topping or sweetened whipped cream. Repeat layers.

Cover with plastic wrap and refrigerate 3 to 4 hours or overnight. When ready to serve, garnish the top with dried cranberries and gingersnap cookies.

Makes 14 servings.

Peppermint Crunch Ice Cream Pie

Sometimes the simplest recipes get the best reviews! Of course, if you're feeling ambitious you can make your own cookie-crumb crust and top the pie with real whipped cream and homemade hot fudge!

1   (1½-quart) package, peppermint ice cream, softened slightly

1   premade Oreo cookie pie crust

    Chocolate fudge ice cream topping, for garnishing

    Non-dairy whipped topping or sweetened whipped cream

    Crushed candy canes, for garnishing

In a large bowl, stir ice cream until softened. Spoon ice cream into pie shell and spread evenly. Freeze 3 to 4 hours, or until solid.

To serve, let pie stand at room temperature about 5 minutes before slicing. Serve topped with fudge topping, whipped cream, and crushed candy canes.

Makes about 6 to 8 servings.

Dutch Apple Pie

Pie is a Christmas tradition at our house, and this pie is one of our favorites. Instead of a flaky pie crust, this crust is more like a big cookie with oats, flour, brown sugar, and butter. This pie is a hit year-round, but it is even more special at Christmastime.

- 1 unbaked 9-inch pie shell, store-bought or homemade
- 5½ cups peeled and sliced Gala apples
- 1 tablespoon lemon juice
- ¾ cup granulated sugar, divided
- ½ cup packed brown sugar, divided
- ¾ cup plus 3 tablespoons all-purpose flour, divided
- 1 teaspoon ground cinnamon
- ¼ teaspoon ground nutmeg
- ⅓ cup butter

Preheat oven to 375 degrees F. Fit pie crust into 9-inch pie plate and set aside.

In a large bowl, toss sliced apples with lemon juice, ½ cup of the granulated sugar, ¼ cup of the brown sugar, 3 tablespoons of the flour, cinnamon, and nutmeg. Pile apples into crust.

In a small bowl blend remaining ¾ cup flour, ¼ cup granulated sugar, ¼ cup brown sugar, and butter with a pastry cutter until coarsely crumbled. Sprinkle crumbs evenly over apples.

Bake 50 minutes, or until top is golden brown and apple filling is sizzling.

Makes 6 to 8 servings.

Almond Joy Bars

These Almond Joy Bars have a delicious graham cracker crust, a creamy coconut filling, and a chocolaty-almond topping. They are absolutely divine and are best served with a tall glass of ice-cold milk. Enjoy!

◇◇◇

- 2 cups finely crushed graham cracker crumbs, about 10 whole graham crackers
- ½ cup butter, melted
- ¼ cup granulated sugar
- 1 (14-ounce) can sweetened condensed milk
- 2 cups sweetened flaked coconut
- 2 cups milk chocolate chips
- ½ tablespoon shortening
- ½ cup chopped almonds

Preheat oven to 350 degrees F.

In a medium bowl, combine crushed graham crackers, melted butter, and sugar. Press mixture into the bottom of a 9x9-inch pan and bake 15 minutes.

Remove partially-baked crust from oven. Combine the condensed milk and coconut flakes in a small bowl. Spread over warm, partially-baked crust, and return to oven an additional 15 minutes, or just until coconut starts to turn golden brown. Remove from oven and place pan on a wire rack.

Melt chocolate chips with vegetable shortening in a microwave-safe bowl on high power for 2 minutes, stopping to stir every 30 seconds. When chocolate is melted and smooth, pour it over the coconut layer and spread evenly. Before the chocolate hardens, sprinkle chopped almonds on top. Let bars cool several hours to set, or refrigerate 20 to 30 minutes for a quicker setting time.

Makes 16 bars.

Peppermint Fudge

Chocolate and peppermint—a match made in heaven! This fudge is easy to whip up and is perfect for any holiday party (or for those days when you're simply having a chocolate-mint craving and need a whole pan for yourself!).

1⅔ cups granulated sugar	1½ cups semisweet chocolate chips
⅔ cup evaporated milk	½ teaspoon vanilla
2 tablespoons butter	¼ teaspoon peppermint extract
¼ teaspoon salt	¼ cup crushed peppermint candy canes
2 cups miniature marshmallows	

Line an 8x8-inch baking pan with aluminum foil and set aside.

In a medium saucepan over medium heat, combine sugar, evaporated milk, butter, and salt. Bring the mixture to a full rolling boil, stirring constantly. Reduce heat to medium-low and continue boiling 4 minutes. Remove saucepan from heat.

Stir in marshmallows, chocolate chips, vanilla, and peppermint extract. Stir quickly for 1 minute, or until marshmallows are completely melted. Pour chocolate mixture into prepared baking pan and let cool 1 to 2 minutes. Top with crushed candy canes, using clean hands to gently press candy into the fudge. Place fudge in the refrigerator and chill 2 hours, or until firm. Lift foil from pan and cut fudge into small pieces. Store up to 3 days in an airtight container in the refrigerator.

Makes 48 pieces.

Baby Ruth Bars

A number of candy bars are severely underrated: Zero bars (have you ever had one of those? If you like white chocolate, they are for you!); Caramello bars (that gooey caramel is heavenly); and, last but not least, Baby Ruth bars! Their peanut-buttery flavor mixed with nougat, caramel, and chocolate is top notch! These homemade bars taste just like their namesake and are a family favorite!

1 cup light corn syrup	6 cups cornflakes cereal
1 cup creamy peanut butter	1½ cups milk chocolate chips, divided
½ cup granulated sugar	⅔ cup roasted peanuts
½ cup packed brown sugar	

Grease 9x13-inch baking pan.

In a large saucepan over medium heat, combine corn syrup, peanut butter, and sugars, stirring until smooth. In a separate bowl, mix together cornflakes, 1 cup of the chocolate chips, and the peanuts. Pour hot corn syrup mixture over the cornflakes mix. Stir until cornflakes are completely coated. Press mixture into a greased baking pan and let cool. When bars are set, melt the remaining ½ cup chocolate chips and drizzle over the bars. Let the chocolate set before serving.

Makes 16 bars.

Mini Turtle Cheesecakes

With an Oreo crust and a classic "turtle" topping, these mini cheesecakes are a smash hit. We doubt you'll be able to eat just one. This recipe makes 48 mini cheesecakes, so you may wish to assemble and bake the cheesecakes in batches.

18 Oreo cookies, finely crushed	1 teaspoon vanilla
3 tablespoons butter, melted	1 teaspoon lemon juice
2 (8-ounce) packages cream cheese, softened	Pecan halves
	Fudge topping
2 eggs	Caramel topping
¾ cup granulated sugar	

Preheat oven to 350 degrees F. Line mini muffin cups with paper liners and set aside.

In a large bowl, mix together Oreos and butter. Press a small spoonful of crumb mixture into the bottom of each liner.

In a separate large bowl, beat together cream cheese, eggs, sugar, vanilla, and lemon juice until light and fluffy. Drop a spoonful of cream cheese mixture into each liner, filling liners almost to the top. Bake 15 minutes.

Remove baked cheesecakes to wire racks to cool completely. Repeat above process until all crumbs and batter have been used.

Once cheesecakes are cooled, remove from cups and place in refrigerator to chill for at least 1 hour. To serve, top each cheesecake with 2 pecan halves, and drizzle with fudge and caramel.

Makes 48 mini cheesecakes.

12
WAYS TO
GIVE BACK

Each holiday season, we try to focus on more than just presents. We have found that we feel the most joy during Christmas when we spend less time thinking about what we want and more time loving and serving those around us. We have rounded up twelve ways you can give back during this time of year. Pick one, two, or all of them! No matter what you choose, we know it will bring a deeper, more meaningful feeling to your Christmas celebrations.

1. **Be a Sub for Santa.** A Sub-for-Santa program does just what it sounds like: provides substitutes for Santa Claus so families who can't afford Christmas can still have presents under their trees. The organization matches children in need to volunteers who can shop for toys, books, clothing, and other gifts that the United Way will then deliver to children ages eighteen months to 14 years. Find your local United Way organization by visiting www.unitedway.org. Organizations in other states provide similar services.

   Of course, you can also create your own Sub-for-Santa event by asking your local church group or another charity organization if there is a family who needs help and then coordinating the purchase and delivery of gifts and food for that family.

2. **Be an Angel.** The Salvation Army's Angel Tree program matches children from qualified families with donors from the local community. Sponsoring companies and groups set up Christmas trees in schools, hospitals, and retail centers throughout the community during the holiday season. The trees are decorated with slips of paper or cards, providing age and gender information about a child in need. Volunteer donors can select a card from the tree and bring back a present! To contact your local Salvation Army, visit www.salvationarmyusa.org and enter your zip code in the search field. A list of local offices will display.

3. **Give Cookies to Heroes.** First responders, such as firemen, police officers, and paramedics are hometown heroes. To thank them for their service, consider delivering cookies to your local fire station or police precinct. Our family has done this the last few years, and it's always so rewarding to give back to these great men and women—especially those who may not get to spend the holidays with their families. We love bringing our Double Chocolate Brownie Cookies.

DOUBLE CHOCOLATE BROWNIE COOKIES

⅔   cup shortening

1   cup packed brown sugar

½ cup granulated sugar

2 eggs

1 teaspoon vanilla

1 tablespoon water

1½ cups all-purpose flour

⅓ cup cocoa powder

¼ teaspoon baking soda

½ teaspoon salt

1 cup milk chocolate chips

1 cup semisweet chocolate chips

Preheat oven to 375 degrees F.

In a large bowl, cream together shortening and sugars. Add eggs, one at a time, mixing well between each egg. Mix in vanilla and water. In a separate bowl, combine flour, cocoa powder, baking soda, and salt. Stir flour mixture into sugar mixture. Do not over mix. Fold in chocolate chips. Drop spoonfuls of dough onto ungreased baking sheets. Bake 7 to 9 minutes. Let cookies cool for a couple of minutes on baking sheet and then move to wire racks to cool completely.

Makes about 2½ dozen cookies.

4. **Pay It Forward.** One day, Kendra went to lunch and when she got up to pay for her meal, someone had already picked up the bill. Her day was made! We all still smile when we think about how great that moment was. Our next step was to pay it forward. Try doing it yourself and see how it makes you feel. There are many ways to do this: at a restaurant, pay for another diner's meal; in the drive-through, pay for the car behind you; in the express lane at the grocery store, pick up the tab of the person in line behind you.

5. **Send a Holiday Treat to the Troops.** Making holiday treats is a fun and rewarding way to give back to the troops who are sacrificing their lives and time away from their families to protect our country.

If you decide to send homemade treats, plan well. Cookies tend to keep better than other treats and are less likely to melt than chocolate candies or fudge. Pack cookies in an airtight plastic container with a slice of bread. The bread will help keep the cookies fresh longer. Consider taping the container shut and then packing it in a box filled with packing peanuts.

Check with your local post office for guidelines on package size, mailing dates, and the policies for shipping perishable goods. Typically, the post office will not accept packages going to military installations overseas later than the first week in December. And guidelines on package size can vary from year to year.

If you'd rather send a basic care package, consider this list of most-requested items:

- Beef jerky
- Canned nuts
- Dried fruit
- Shaving cream
- White or green socks
- Sudoku or crossword puzzle books
- Hot chocolate packets
- Chewing gum

6. **Make a Ring-and-Run Christmas Dinner.** Every year on Christmas Eve, our family delivers the fixings for a Christmas dinner to a family in need. We love to just leave the box on the doorstep, ring the bell and then run. It always feels so good to anticipate a family's reaction to the Christmas surprise. In the past we've obtained the name of a family from a local church leader who has a good idea of what's going on in the community and who could use some help. Our "dinner box" typically includes a giant turkey, a bag of rolls, a box of stuffing mix, a bowl of mashed potatoes (or potato pearls), gravy, all the fixings for green bean casserole, and a dessert, such as our Rocky Road Brownies.

ROCKY ROAD BROWNIES

8	tablespoons cocoa powder
1	cup margarine or butter, melted
2	cups granulated sugar
4	eggs
1	teaspoon vanilla
2½	cups all-purpose flour

	Pinch salt
1	cup milk chocolate chips
1	cup chopped nuts
1	(10-ounce) bag mini marshmallows
1	recipe Chocolate Drizzle (see recipe below)

Preheat oven to 325 degrees F. Coat a 9x13-inch baking pan with nonstick cooking spray.

In a large bowl, stir together melted margarine and cocoa. Add sugar and eggs and mix well. Stir in vanilla, flour, and salt. Bake 20 to 25 minutes, until a toothpick inserted into the center comes out clean.

Remove brownies from oven and top with chocolate chips, marshmallows, and chopped nuts. Return to oven for about 3 minutes, or until the marshmallows double in size. Remove from oven and let cool. Top with Chocolate Drizzle and serve.

Makes about 2 dozen brownies.

CHOCOLATE DRIZZLE

¼	cup butter, melted
1	cup powdered sugar
1½	teaspoons cocoa powder

In a small bowl, beat together all ingredients. If the drizzle seems too thick, add a little milk to thin. If it's too thin, add a little more powdered sugar.

7. **Volunteer at a Local Soup Kitchen.** There are many places in your community or city looking for extra hands to help feed the homeless during the holidays. Only a few hours of your time can have a big impact on the people you serve. To find a local soup kitchen or food pantry, do a Google search with those terms and the name of your town or community. Or, visit www.volunteermatch.org, where you can enter the name of your city and a way you'd like to help to find organizations that match what you are looking for.

8. **Donate to Local Drives.** There are many community donation drives that occur during the holiday season. Local grocery stores, schools, hospitals, and other businesses often have donation boxes for items such as coats, mittens, shoes, toys, and packaged foods. Make it fun by involving the entire family in selecting a local cause and providing donations. You can find some good information at www.Charity Navigator.org.

9. **Give Thanks.** Christmas is a time to remember family, friends, and loved ones. What better way to spread love and holiday spirit than by expressing gratitude? You can send a thank-you note to a former teacher, coach, or church leader. Write an email to a colleague, a handwritten note to an elderly acquaintance or neighbor, or just take a few minutes to call a loved one. They may be inspired to do the same for someone they appreciate. Saying "thank you" is another simple way to express gratitude. Make it a point to be gracious and kind to everyone you meet.

10. **Get Your Hands Dirty.** We grew up with a lot of snow in Utah. It was always nice to come home to a shoveled driveway after a big snowstorm. Even if you live in a warm area, you could help with some form of yard work, take in a neighbor's garbage can, or bring the newspaper to an elderly neighbor's front porch. Christmas is a great time to be especially mindful of those who might be spending the holidays alone or find it difficult to shovel their own walks or get out and shop for Christmas.

11. **Open Your Home.** Many people who are far from home miss out on the family activities that make the holidays fun and memorable. Whether it is for friends, family, neighbors, or coworkers, an invitation to a family dinner or game night during the month of December would be greatly appreciated by someone who may have no one else to share the season with. It doesn't need to be an elaborate occasion, just welcome them with open heart and home.

12. **Search for Service.** Sometimes the best forms of service are right in front of our faces; they often go unnoticed. You could pull over and help a stranded car in the snow or help an elderly neighbor hang up Christmas lights. Make a double batch of cookies and take the extras to someone who needs a lift. Offer to babysit for a busy mother. Write a secret "thank you" or "I love you" note to a family member. It doesn't always have to cost money to serve; it just takes time.

12
GIFTS FOR
NEIGHBORS

Here are twelve fun ideas for neighbor gifts. Each idea is relatively simple and can be "dressed up" by adding ribbon, bows, clever notes, or coordinating accessories.

1. **Box of Nuts.** Fill your home with a spicy, cinnamon-vanilla scent while making these easy neighbor gifts. After the nuts have cooked and cooled, transfer to clear bags or decorative boxes and tie with a Christmas ribbon or tulle bow.

SLOW-COOKER CINNAMON ALMONDS

- 1 cup granulated sugar
- 1 cup brown sugar
- 3 tablespoons ground cinnamon
- ⅛ teaspoon salt
- 1 egg white
- 2 teaspoons vanilla
- 3 cups whole almonds
- 2 tablespoons water

In a medium bowl, combine sugars, cinnamon, and salt; set aside. In a separate bowl, whisk together egg white and vanilla until frothy. Stir in almonds to coat. Add almonds to cinnamon-sugar mixture and toss until completely coated.

Spray slow cooker with nonstick cooking spray. Add almonds and cook on high for 2 hours, stirring every 20 minutes. After 2 hours, pour water over the almonds and mix very well to make sure there are no clumps. Reduce heat to low and cook 1 more hour, continuing to stir every 20 minutes. Line a cookie sheet with parchment paper and spread out the almonds to cool and dry on the paper.

2. **Refrigerated Cookie Dough.** Skip a step in the cookie-baking process and package up the dough instead! Make your own dough and package in plastic tubs, or use tubes of store-bought dough. If you make your own dough, remember to add directions for storing and baking the dough.

- Refrigerated cookie dough, homemade or store-bought
- Ribbon
- Gift tags

Tie a ribbon around the packaged cookie dough and attach a gift tag that reads:

"With so many holiday treats
And everyone on the go,
Here is something quick and sweet
To cook—or just eat the dough!"

3. **Tasty Turtle Bites.** These easy-to-make, bite-sized sweets are something your whole family can help put together. Kids will love opening the Rolo Caramels and assembling the treats. Once the pretzel bites cool, stick them in a cute little bag, tie with a ribbon, and deliver to your neighbors. For a nut-free version, replace pecan halves with M&M's candies and use Hershey's Kisses instead of Rolo Caramels.

ROLO PRETZEL TURTLE BITES

1   (11-ounce) bag Rolo Caramels in Milk Chocolate, unwrapped

½   pound pecan halves

50   mini pretzels

Preheat oven to 350 degrees F. Line a baking sheet with parchment paper.

Line pretzels across prepared baking sheet. Top each pretzel with 1 Rolo caramel. Carefully transfer baking sheet to hot oven and cook 3 to

4 minutes. Remove from oven and gently press a pecan half on top of each Rolo. Let pretzel bites set up before packaging.

4. **Spicy Salsa.** This zesty, homemade salsa comes together quickly, but you can use jars of store-bought salsa if you're short on time. To package the gift, tie a ribbon around the jar and attach a note. Deliver with a bag of tortilla chips.

EASY BLENDER SALSA

2   (14.5-ounce) cans whole tomatoes, drained

3 to 4   whole canned jalapeños (not pickled)

1   yellow onion, peeled and quartered

1   teaspoon garlic salt

½   teaspoon salt

1   teaspoon cumin

½   teaspoon granulated sugar

2   teaspoons lime juice

Place all ingredients in a blender or food processor and puree until smooth. Transfer to clean mason jars, screw on lids, and add this Christmas greeting: "Just a little something to spice up your holiday season!" Salsa will stay fresh for one week in the refrigerator.

5. **Root Beer Reindeer.** These cute "reindeer" can be given in 6 packs to neighbor families or as individual bottles to your kids' friends or teachers at school.

- 9 brown pipe cleaners
- 1 six-pack IBC Root Beer
- 12 (15-milimeter) googly eyes
- 6 (½-inch) red craft pom-poms
- Hot glue
- Gift tags

Cut 3 pipe cleaners in half, and then cut those halves in half to make 12 quarter-length pieces; set aside. Wrap 1 full-length pipe cleaner around each bottle, just below the cap. Twist the pipe cleaner in the back of the bottle and bring the ends up on each side to make antlers. Twist 1 quarter-length pipe cleaner around each main antler, about 1 inch from the top to make "branches" on the antlers.

Glue 2 googly eyes on each bottle's neck, about 1½ inches below the cap. Glue 1 pom-pom beneath each set of eyes.

Attach a gift tag to the 6-pack that reads: "We're rooting for you to have a very Merry Christmas!"

6. **Paper Plates.** No one wants to wash dishes during the crazy holiday season. Give the gift of more time by packaging paper plates to give as neighbor gifts. You might want to save a stack for yourself, as well!

- Paper plates
- Ribbon
- Gift tags

Divide paper plates into stacks. Tie each stack with a ribbon and attach a gift tag that reads: "Our Christmas wish to you—fewer dishes to do!"

7. **Light up the Season.** Use light as a gift-giving theme. This can be practical (by gifting a flashlight or light bulbs) or fun (by gifting a box of Christmas lights or a light-up ornament).

- Flashlight, light bulbs, or a box of Christmas lights
- Ribbon
- Gift tags

Tie a ribbon around your gift of "light" and attach a gift tag with this note: "May your days be happy, your heart be light, your Christmas merry, and the New Year bright!"

8. **A Measure of Joy.** This simple idea is perfect for neighbors and friends who love to bake.

- 1 set measuring cups or spoons
- Ribbon
- Gift tags

Thread ribbon through measuring cups or spoons and attach a gift tag that reads: "Wishing you joy beyond measure this holiday season!"

9. **Fake Fudge.** Some years, there just isn't time to whip up batches and batches of fudge. Simple gifts like this are perfect for those times.

- Giant candy bars
- Ribbon
- Gift tags

Tie a ribbon around a few giant candy bars and attach a gift tag with this poem:

"A day or two ago,
We thought we'd make a treat
For all our special friends,
A Christmas treat to eat.
Our intentions were top-notch
But our schedules wouldn't budge.
Hence, here's this year's edition
Of homemade Christmas Fudge!"

10. **A Great Match.** This is another practical gift for friends and neighbors. Keep it simple, as described below. Or embellish the gift with a bag of marshmallows and a set of roasting sticks.

   • Box of matches, regular or long reaching

   • Ribbon

   • Gift tags

   Tie a ribbon around the box of matches and attach a note that reads: "No one matches you as neighbors! Merry Christmas!"

11. **A Treat of Truffles.** These truffles will win rave reviews from your neighbors. Pile them up on a plate or place them in a decorative gift box, topped with a bow.

HOMEMADE PEANUT BUTTER TRUFFLES

1	cup butter, softened
1	pound powdered sugar
1	cup creamy peanut butter
10 to 12	whole graham crackers, finely crushed
2	pounds dipping chocolate, such as Wilton Light Cocoa Candy Melts or Guittard Milk Chocolate Apeels, melted

In a large bowl, mix together butter, powdered sugar, peanut butter, and graham crackers crumbs. Roll dough in to 1-inch balls and place on a parchment-lined cookie sheet. Freeze 20 minutes. In the meantime, melt dipping chocolate according to package directions. Once the peanut butter balls have set up, dip each ball in chocolate and then return to cookie sheet. Let set up before serving/sharing with neighbors.

Makes 6 to 7 dozen truffles.

12. **Ready-to-Eat Rolls.** There's nothing like piping-hot rolls fresh from the oven. Of course, if you're delivering rolls to neighbors, those rolls aren't going to stay warm as you go from door to door. Instead, try this gift and let your neighbors raise and bake the rolls themselves.

   • Frozen roll dough, such as Rhodes

   • Ribbon

   • Gift tags

   Tie a ribbon around the bag of rolls and attach a gift card that reads:

   "Here's a little holiday treat.
   Rise and bake, it can't be beat!
   Warm, fresh rolls just for you.
   Top with butter, that's all you do!"

Slow-Cooker Ham with Honey Mustard Glaze

This ham has only a few ingredients and requires very little preparation. If you're feeding a crowd this Christmas and want to serve something that tastes like you spent all day in the kitchen, this is the dish!

1 (7- to 10-pound) fully cooked, bone-in ham

1 cup brown sugar

1 cup honey

½ cup Dijon mustard

¼ cup apple juice

Spray slow cooker with nonstick cooking spray. Remove skin and excess fat from ham. Make surface cuts in ham about an inch apart and ¼-inch deep in a diamond pattern on top of the ham. Place ham in slow cooker. In a small bowl, combine brown sugar, honey, Dijon mustard, and apple juice. Brush glaze over ham. Cover slow cooker with lid and warm ham on low 8 to 10 hours.

If your ham is too large to use the slow cooker lid, use aluminum foil to make a tent for the ham. Cover foil with a towel and cook as directed.

Makes 10 to 12 servings.

Slow-Cooker Ham and Pineapple Sandwiches

You've probably guessed by now that slow cookers are one of our secrets to a successful dinner during the holidays. The pineapple and ham in this dish complement each other perfectly, and when they cook together in the slow cooker all day, it's a home run.

4	cups chopped, cooked ham	¼	cup minced onions
1	(20-ounce) can crushed pineapple	¼	cup Dijon mustard
¾	cup brown sugar	10 to 12	hamburger buns
1	medium green bell pepper, diced	10 to 12	slices Swiss cheese

Coat slow cooker with nonstick cooking spray.

Add first 6 ingredients to the slow cooker and stir together. Cook on low 3 to 4 hours, or until completely heated through.

When ready to serve, preheat broiler to high. Scoop sandwich filling on one half of a large hamburger or sandwich bun. Top filling with a slice of Swiss cheese and place on a broiler-safe baking sheet. Repeat for each sandwich.

Place baking sheet under broiler until cheese is melted and bubbly, about 1 to 2 minutes. Remove from broiler and top each sandwich with remaining bun halves.

Makes 10 to 12 sandwiches.

Slow-Cooker Balsamic Pot Roast

This is one of the most tender and juicy pot roasts you'll ever taste, and the flavor from the herbs and balsamic vinegar is divine!

2 tablespoons olive oil

1 (3- to 4-pound) boneless beef chuck roast

Salt and pepper to taste

1 pound baby carrots

3 ribs celery, chopped into large pieces

1 onion, sliced

½ cup balsamic vinegar

1 cup tomato juice

1 (14.5-ounce) can beef broth

3 cloves garlic, minced

1 teaspoon dried thyme

½ teaspoon ground sage

2 bay leaves

3 tablespoons cornstarch

3 tablespoons cold water

Heat olive oil in a large skillet over medium-high heat. Season roast with salt and pepper to taste and place in skillet and sear on all sides. Remove from skillet and place in a slow cooker coated with nonstick cooking spray.

Cover roast with carrots, celery, and onions. In a small bowl, mix together balsamic vinegar, tomato juice, beef broth, garlic, thyme, and sage. Pour over the roast. Place 2 bay leaves on top and cover with lid. Cook on low at least 9 to 10 hours.

When done cooking, remove roast and vegetables and keep warm. Skim the fat off the liquid and pour liquid into a saucepan. In a small bowl, mix together the corn starch and cold water; pour into the saucepan and mix well. Place saucepan on stove top and heat over medium-high heat until it starts to boil. Let cook for about 2 minutes, or until it starts to thicken. Serve gravy with pot roast and vegetables.

Makes 6 to 8 servings.

Slow-Cooker Chicken and Gravy

This meal takes only a few minutes to throw in the slow cooker and is perfect for those busy days during the holiday season. If desired, use the broth to make your own gravy at the end instead of using a mix.

6   large, boneless, skinless chicken breasts

4   cups fat-free chicken broth

4   (0.87-ounce) packages chicken gravy mix

Place chicken breasts in the bottom of the slow cooker. Pour in chicken broth. If broth doesn't cover the chicken, add a little bit of water. Cook on low 8 hours, or high 4 to 5 hours.

Pour 4 cups of the broth and chicken juices from the slow cooker into a small saucepan. Add 4 packages gravy mix and stir, over medium-high heat, until thickened, about 2 minutes.

Remove chicken from the slow cooker and shred with 2 forks. Add shredded chicken to the gravy and stir to combine well. Serve over mashed potatoes or noodles. Add salt and pepper to taste.

Makes 6 servings.

Slow-Cooker Chicken Fajita Soup

You can put this recipe together in the morning, go Christmas shopping all afternoon, wrap presents in the evening, and sit down to a delicious dinner that night!

- 1 pound boneless, skinless chicken breasts
- 2 (10.75-ounce) cans condensed cream of chicken soup
- 1 cup salsa
- 2 cups frozen corn
- 1 (15-ounce) can black beans, drained and rinsed

- 1½ cups water
- 1 teaspoon ground cumin
- ½ teaspoon dried cilantro (optional)
- 1 cup shredded cheddar cheese

  Favorite toppings, such as sour cream, tomatoes, green onions, lettuce

Coat slow cooker with nonstick cooking spray. Place chicken into slow cooker.

In a bowl, mix together cream of chicken soup, salsa, corn, black beans, water, cumin, and cilantro. Pour over chicken in slow cooker. Cook on low 4 to 6 hours. Remove chicken and shred using 2 forks. Put chicken back into slow cooker, add cheese, and let cook 15 more minutes. Serve with your favorite fajita toppings.

Makes 4 to 5 servings.

Slow-Cooker Texas Chili

Everyone loves a warm bowl of chili on a cold night! When we were growing up, Mom would make this throughout wintertime. It's absolutely perfect for the busy holiday season: dump everything in the slow cooker, and you have a delicious meal just a few hours later.

1 pound ground beef

1 large onion, diced

2 green bell peppers, diced

1 (4-ounce) can diced green chili peppers

1 (14-ounce) can beef broth

1 (15-ounce) can pinto beans, drained and rinsed

1 (14-ounce) can diced tomatoes, undrained

2 (8-ounce) cans tomato sauce

1 (6-ounce) can tomato paste

3 cloves garlic, minced

1 tablespoon ground cumin

2 tablespoons chili powder

1 tablespoon granulated sugar

1 teaspoon salt

1 teaspoon ground black pepper

Pinch red pepper flakes (optional)

In a large skillet over medium heat, brown ground beef and diced onion until meat is no longer pink and onion is tender. Add to slow cooker. Dump remaining ingredients on top and cook on low 4 to 6 hours (it really could go as long as 8 hours on low if you need it to). Serve with shredded cheese, sour cream, green onions, and a bag of Fritos corn chips, or any of your other favorite toppings!

Makes 6 to 8 servings.

Citrus-Glazed Salmon

This orange-infused salmon will make everyone at your table smile. The orange marmalade spread gives it just the right amount of tanginess, for a quick and easy meal your whole family is bound to love.

4 (6-ounce) salmon fillets	½ teaspoon garlic powder
½ cup orange marmalade	¼ teaspoon ground black pepper
1 tablespoon Dijon mustard	⅛ teaspoon ground ginger
½ teaspoon salt	

Preheat your oven's broiler to high. Line a broiler-safe baking dish with foil and coat with nonstick cooking spray.

Place salmon in prepared baking dish. In a small bowl, combine remaining ingredients to make a glaze. Reserve a small amount of glaze. Baste each salmon filet with a generous amount of glaze and broil 4 minutes. Remove salmon from under the broiler, turn over, baste with glaze, and return to the oven 4 more minutes. Remove the salmon from under the broiler and serve with reserved glaze.

Makes 4 servings.

Applesauce Pork Tenderloin

This moist, flavorful pork loin will have all your dinner guests wanting seconds!

◇◇◇

- 1 (2-pound) pork tenderloin
- ½ teaspoon salt
- ¼ teaspoon black pepper
- 2 tablespoons vegetable oil
- 1 cup applesauce
- ½ cup brown sugar
- 3 tablespoons Dijon mustard
- 2 tablespoons honey
- 2 sprigs fresh rosemary, roughly chopped

Preheat oven to 350 degrees F.

Sprinkle tenderloin with salt and pepper. In a large skillet, heat vegetable oil over medium-high heat. Sear tenderloin on all sides. Place tenderloin in a shallow roasting pan. Combine applesauce, brown sugar, mustard, and honey and spread over tenderloin. Top with rosemary and bake, uncovered, 1 to 1¼ hours, until internal temperature reaches 145 degrees F. on a meat thermometer.

Makes 8 to 10 servings.

Sticky Sesame Chicken

You can't go wrong with this recipe, which is a comforting thought during the holiday season! It is simple but delicious and can easily be doubled or tripled to feed bigger crowds.

1½ to 2 pounds frozen popcorn chicken

6 tablespoons honey

4 tablespoons ketchup

4 tablespoons granulated sugar

2 tablespoons white distilled vinegar

2 tablespoons soy sauce

Salt and pepper, to taste

Green onions, chopped, for garnishing

Sesame seeds, for garnishing

6 cups cooked rice

Cook popcorn chicken according to package directions. In a saucepan over medium heat, whisk together honey, ketchup, sugar, vinegar, soy sauce, and salt and pepper. Bring sauce to a boil while stirring, reduce heat, and simmer a few minutes until sauce slightly thickens. Toss cooked chicken in sauce and serve over rice. Garnish with green onion and sesame seeds.

Makes 4 to 6 servings.

Grandma's Meatloaf

This recipe has been in our family for years and is one of our favorites. It is our grandma's recipe; and she is *the* meatloaf expert. It's a quick and hearty meal that can be prepared ahead of time or right before cooking.

1½ pounds ground beef

2 eggs

1 small onion, chopped

¼ cup ketchup

Salt and pepper, to taste

1 cup oatmeal

1 (10.75-ounce) can tomato soup, divided

2 tablespoons Worcestershire sauce, divided

2 tablespoons brown sugar

Preheat oven to 350 degrees F.

In a large bowl, use clean hands to combine beef, eggs, onion, ketchup, salt and pepper, oatmeal, half of the soup, and 1 tablespoon Worcestershire sauce. Mold mixture and move to a 9x5 loaf pan. In a small bowl, stir together brown sugar, remaining Worcestershire sauce, and remaining soup and pour over top of loaf. Bake 90 minutes, or until internal temperature reaches 160 degrees F.

Makes 8 servings.

Perfect Fried Pork Chops

Pork chops were one of our family favorites when we were little. These pork chops are full of flavor and are so easy to make!

8 pieces very thin bone-in pork chops	1 teaspoon steak seasoning
1 teaspoon seasoned salt	½ cup canola oil
1 teaspoon black pepper	1 tablespoon butter
½ cup all-purpose flour	

Rinse pork chops and pat dry with paper towels. Salt and pepper both sides of the pork chops.

In a small bowl, combine flour and steak seasoning. Dip each side of the pork chops in the flour mixture, then set aside on a plate.

In a heavy skillet, heat canola oil over medium to medium-high heat. Add butter. When butter is melted and oil mixture is hot, cook chops 2 to 3 minutes on the first side. Flip and cook 1 to 2 minutes on the other side. Remove to a plate and repeat with remaining pork chops. A meat thermometer should register 145 degrees F. when chops are done.

Makes 8 servings.

Chicken Taco Casserole

This recipe is something you can throw together when you are short on time but still want to feed your family something yummy. Kids love it too!

2 (10.75-ounce) cans cream of chicken soup

1½ cups sour cream

1 (14-ounce) can Ro-Tel or diced tomatoes with green chilies

1 (15-ounce) can black beans, drained and rinsed

1 (1-ounce) packet taco seasoning

3 cups cooked and shredded chicken

1 (10-ounce) bag tortilla chips, crushed

2 cups shredded cheddar cheese

Preheat oven to 350 degrees F. Lightly grease a 9x13-inch pan.

In a large bowl, combine the chicken soup, sour cream, Ro-Tel, black beans, taco seasoning, and chicken. Set aside.

Spread half of the crushed tortilla chips over the bottom of the prepared pan. Spread half of the chicken mixture over the chips. Top with 1 cup of the cheese. Repeat layers.

Bake 30 minutes, until bubbly and cheese starts to brown.

Serve with your favorite taco toppings (sour cream, lettuce, tomatoes, salsa, guacamole, and so on).

Makes 6 servings.

12

HOMEMADE CHRISTMAS GIFTS

Handmade gifts are not only beautiful, they are also special. They let the ones you love know how much you appreciate them. Homemade gifts, whether large or small, help us remember what Christmas is all about.

1. **GLASS VASE CHRISTMAS LUMINARIES**

These easy-to-make Christmas Luminaries are perfect for brightening a cold winter's night. This would be a great gift for a mom, grandma, or friend.

- Glass vases, assorted sizes and styles
- Twine or yarn
- Masking tape
- Spray paint, any light color (Almond Satin is shown here)
- LED tea lights

※ Tape one end of the twine to the underside of a vase. Wrap the twine up and down around the vase several times.

※ Tape the end of the twine on the inside of the vase. (Don't put the masking tape on the outside of the vase. It will leave a tape outline behind after spray painting.)

※ Coat the vase twice with spray paint. Let the paint dry then remove the twine and tape.

※ Place an LED tea light inside each vase for a beautiful, glowing luminary.

2. T-SHIRT SUPERHERO CAPE

A personalized superhero cape will help your child's imagination soar to new heights. This cape can be made from an old T-shirt and doesn't involve any sewing. Even better, whoever receives it is likely to think you're the superhero!

- Large adult T-shirt
- Chalk or fabric pencil (optional)
- Scissors
- Hot glue
- Velcro
- Patches or iron-on decals

❋ Lay the T-shirt face up on a flat surface.

❋ Remove the sleeves by cutting along the inside of the seam lines.

❋ Cut up both sides seams of the T-shirt to the armpit. Open the shirt and lay it flat on a table. The neck hole should be in the middle.

❋ Starting from one shoulder, cut on the seam line around the back of the of the shirt, following the collar, and through the other shoulder. What remains should be the shirt's collar and the cape in the front.

❋ Because you will have used a large T-shirt, the collar will need to be trimmed to better fit around your child's neck. Snip the collar in the middle front and then trim a little from each side until the length seems appropriate.

❋ Use hot glue to attach Velcro to each side of the collar.

❋ Decorate the cape using patches or iron-on decals of your child's favorite things, such as a basketball or princess crown.

3. BURLAP HANDPRINT TREE SKIRT

This is a great gift for the mom or grandma who has everything. The little handprints add the perfect touch to show it really was handmade.

- 2½ square yards burlap (90x90 inches)
- Iron
- Chalk or fabric pencil
- Yardstick or tape measurer
- Hot glue gun and glue sticks
- Black acrylic paint
- Paper plate
- Foam paint brush

✳ Fold the burlap in half. Iron along the fold to smooth and flatten the fabric. Lay the fabric on a table with the fold at the top.

✳ Starting at the left end of the fold, use a yardstick to measure in and then mark the 45-inch point. This is the center of the fabric.

✳ From the center point, measure 36 inches and mark along the folded edge.

✳ Rotate the yardstick a few inches and again measure out 36 inches and mark that point. Repeat until the marks form a half circle below the fold.

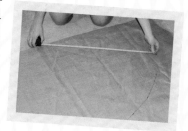

✳ Use chalk or a fabric marker to connect the dots and make a line to cut along.

✳ The next step is to make a smaller circle in the middle, where the tree will go. This circle should be at least 6 inches in diameter but may need to be larger, depending on the size of the tree's trunk. Starting at the center point, measure straight to the right at least 3 inches (increase the length for a larger opening). Mark that point.

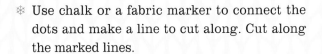

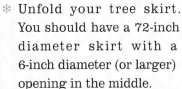

✳ Rotate the yardstick and continue measuring out and marking 3 inches (or the longer length used in the previous step) from the center point until the dots form a small half circle below the fold.

✳ Use chalk or a fabric marker to connect the dots and make a line to cut along. Cut along the marked lines.

✳ Unfold your tree skirt. You should have a 72-inch diameter skirt with a 6-inch diameter (or larger) opening in the middle.

✳ Use the yardstick to mark and then cut along a straight line from the opening in the middle down to the outer edge of the skirt.

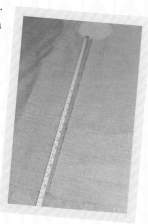

* Cut leftover burlap into 2-inch wide strips of varying lengths.

* Attach strips with hot glue to the edge of the tree skirt to make ruffles that circle the skirt.

* Squirt paint onto a paper plate and spread around with a foam brush.

* Have your children place their hands in the paint and then press them into the tree skirt to decorate.

* Use fabric paint to let each child write his or her name next to the handprints.

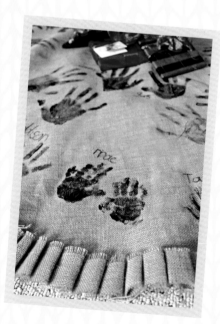

4. PERSONALIZED BOOKS ON CD

Being far away from family can be hard during the holidays. Receiving a book and its recording from an aunt or grandparent would be the perfect gift for any child! It is an easy gift to make and a special way to stay connected to your loved ones far away. If your computer system does not have a CD or DVD drive, consider making an MP3. When you send the book to the child, include a note that asks the child to email you for a surprise addition to the book. When you get the email, reply by sending the digital file back to the child.

- Children's book
- CD-ROM and case
- CD burner program, such as Windows Sound Recorder or QuickTime for Mac
- Microphone, if your computer does not have one built in
- Permanent marker

* Practice reading the book several times before recording. Consider adding sound effects to indicate when to turn the page or to make the recording more fun.

* Insert CD in your computer's DVD or CD-ROM drive.

* Open your system's sound recording application and follow the directions for making a recording.

* Burn the recording to the CD.

* Remove the CD from the drive and use a permanent marker to label the CD with the name of the book.

* Wrap the book and CD together and send to the child.

5. WOOD PHOTO BLOCKS

Turn a simple photograph into a work of art by using Mod Podge to make these fun Wood Photo Blocks. If you are making multiple blocks, consider going to a hardware store and having them cut an 8-foot 2x4 into 6-inch blocks.

- 4x6-inch printed photos, matte finish
- 6-inch 2x4 wood blocks
- 80-grit sandpaper
- Cloth rags
- 120-grit sandpaper (optional)
- Black acrylic paint
- Foam paint brush
- Mod Podge

* Using 80-grit sandpaper, sand the blocks well to smooth off all rough edges.

* Wipe off saw dust with a clean rag and, if desired, use 120-grit sandpaper to smooth out block a second time. Wipe off any dust.

* Paint the blocks using quick, swift motions. The block should look distressed and doesn't need to be completely covered.

* Let the paint dry. If desired, use 120-grit sandpaper to distress the paint. Wipe clean.

* Using your hands, tear all four edges of the photo to give it a ragged, white outline.

* Apply a thin coat of Mod Podge to the side of the block where you will attach the picture. Make sure it is completely covered.

* Place the photo on top of the Mod Podge before it dries, pressing down well to remove any air bubbles.

* Once the picture and Mod Podge are dry, cover the photo with a thin coat of Mod Podge and let it dry.

6. DIY BLEACH T-SHIRTS

Everyone loves T-shirts. Getting a T-shirt that is designed especially for you is such a fun gift! Kids can easily help with this project. For your design, pick something relatively simple, as it will have to be cut out precisely with an X-Acto knife. When choosing a color for your shirt, consider searching online to know what happens to certain colors when bleached. For example, the bleached portion of a black T-shirt will turn a peachy-orange color.

- T-shirt design
- Freezer paper
- Pencil
- X-Acto knife
- Scissors
- Colored T-shirt
- Cardboard
- Spray bottle
- Bleach
- Water

❋ Look online for a simple design, or make your own with letters and clip art. Remember that the design will need to be cut very precisely, so the more intricate it is, the more difficult it will be to cut out.

❋ Print the design.

❋ Trace your design onto the paper side of the freezer paper (not the shiny, waxy side).

❋ Use an X-Acto knife to carefully cut out the design.

❋ Place the design on the T-shirt, shiny side down. Make sure the shiny side of the paper is facing down and that the design is positioned exactly where you want it.

❋ Iron the design onto the T-shirt. The wax on the shiny side will melt and cause the freezer paper to stick to the T-shirt but easily pull off when finished.

❋ Take the shirt outside to the sidewalk or driveway and place a piece of cardboard between the layers of the shirt so it's positioned under the freezer paper and the design won't "leak" on to the back of the shirt.

❋ Fill a water bottle with 3 parts bleach and 1 part water. Spray the bleach-water solution all over the front of your shirt.

❋ Certain colors, like black, will instantly change color. Red-colored shirts can take up to 20 minutes before you see a change.

❋ Let the shirt sit for about 30 minutes,

and then remove the cardboard and peel off the freezer paper.

※ Rinse the shirt thoroughly in the bathtub.

※ Wash and dry the shirt before wearing.

7. EASY INFINITY SCARF

This easy gift just needs a length of scrap material and a few stitches on your sewing machine. You can cut your fabric to the dimensions listed here or experiment with different lengths and widths.

- Scrap fabric, about 18 inches wide by 4 feet long
- Pins
- Thread
- Needle
- Sewing machine
- Scissors

※ Lay the fabric on a flat surface, right-side up.

※ Fold the fabric in half lengthwise and line up the raw edges. The right side of the fabric will be inside.

※ Sew the raw edges together. Turn your scarf inside out so the frayed edges are on the inside.

※ Lay out the scarf with the seam facing up in the center. Fold the scarf in half lengthwise so the frayed edges line up at the top.

※ Sew the frayed edges on the top using a straight stitch. Then stitch over the edges with a zigzag stitch so it won't fray. The seam will be on the back of your scarf so it won't be visible.

8. HINGE BRACELET

Stumped about what to give a girl who loves jewelry but has so much of it you're worried about buying something she already owns? This Hinge Bracelet is perfect. It is so unique that no other girl will have anything like it!

- 2 packages of 1-inch door hinges (8 hinges per packet)
- Newspaper
- Spray paint
- Thin elastic jewelry cord
- Scissors

* Lay hinges on top of a sheet of newspaper.

* Coat the fronts of the hinges with spray paint and let them dry.

* When the front sides are dry, flip hinges over and spray the back sides.

* Let the back sides dry and then add a second coat of spray paint.

* When back sides are dry, flip hinges over and coat the front sides a second time.

* Let hinges dry. Line up the painted hinges so the holes on the right side of each hinge are overlapped by the holes on the left side of the next hinge. This will help you remember how to position the hinges as you thread them on. Line up as many hinges as needed to make the bracelet the appropriate length. (Use a string to measure your recipient's wrist—or the wrist of someone similarly sized.)

* Cut a long piece of elastic jewelry cord. Working from the back side to the front side, thread cord through the overlapping holes on the bottom of the first two hinges.

* Thread the cord through the top hole of the overlapping hinges from front to back so the two are now joined together.

* Pick up the next hinge and hold it in position (the holes on its left side overlapping the holes on the right side of the hinge to the left).

* From the backside, thread the cord up through the bottom set of overlapping holes. (The cord will have been pulled diagonally to reach the bottom set.)

* Thread the cord back down through the top set of holes. Repeat for remaining hinges. Follow the same process to join the first hinge to the last hinge and close the circle.

* Finish off by tying a square knot on the inside of the bracelet after pulling the cord through the last set of holes.

9. T-SHIRT HEADBAND

This T-Shirt headband dresses up a ponytail in a matter of seconds and is very comfortable to wear. It works great for children and adults and is very easy to make with one of your kid's old T-shirts.

- T-shirt
- Scissors
- Elastic headband
- Hot glue gun and glue sticks

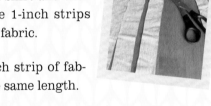

❊ Cut the bottom hem off of your T-shirt and then cut three 1-inch strips from the fabric.

❊ Trim each strip of fabric to the same length.

❊ Put a dab of glue at the top of the first strip and then glue the second strip on top of the first.

❊ Put a dab of glue on the second strip and then glue the third strip on top of that.

❊ Once glue dries, braid the three pieces together and use hot glue to secure the ends.

❊ Set the braid aside. Cut a 2- to 4-inch piece from the elastic headband. The length depends on the size of your head.

❊ Glue one end of the elastic strip to the backside of one end of the headband.

❊ Use hot glue to attach the other end of the braid to the other end of the elastic.

❊ Cut a small strip of fabric from the T-shirt and wrap the unfinished edges and attach with hot glue.

10. RECIPE BINDER

This idea was inspired by Mom because she loves ripping recipes out of magazines or printing them off the Internet. There usually isn't any order to her loose recipes. It's a fun gift to make and would be perfect for almost anyone. The kids could easily help, too.

- 7 to 8 tabbed dividers
- Pen or Sharpie
- 1 box sheet protectors
- 1 presentation-view 3-ring binder
- Colorful paper for the front cover

❋ Begin by labeling your tabs. Simply use a pen or Sharpie to write recipe categories on the inserts that come with a set of tabs. Make a tab for each of the following (or create your own) categories: appetizers, breads, main dishes, side dishes, desserts, drinks, holidays.

❋ Place dividers in binder, along with 5 or 6 sheet protectors per section. Place any extra sheet protectors in the back of the binder.

❋ Have your kids make a cover on colorful paper and insert it in the plastic cover on the front of the binder.

11. PHOTO CLOCK

A special photo of an important event like a wedding, anniversary, graduation, or birthday is the perfect kind of picture to turn into a clock.

Any sister, aunt, grandma, or friend would love something homemade that holds meaning to them.

- 1 (6x8-inch) piece wood, cut ½ inch thick.
- Fine-grit sand paper
- Foam paintbrush
- Black paint (or whatever color you would like)
- Mod Podge
- 1 (4x6-inch) matte photograph
- Drill
- Clock mechanism (you can find one at any craft store)
- Picture hanger or stand

❋ Sand the wood until all rough edges are smooth.

❋ Paint wood with at least 2 coats of black paint, letting it dry between each coat.

❋ Lay your picture on the wood and position it where you want your clock to be.

❋ Mark the picture and the wood so you know where to drill the hole for your clock.

❋ Take the picture off and drill the hole. Keep making the hole bigger until the clock will fit snugly.

* Lay your picture over the wood and cut a small hole in the picture so the clock will fit through it.

* Remove the picture and paint a thin layer of Mod Podge on the wood.

* Carefully place your picture back on and smooth it out. Press your hand hard against the picture starting in the middle and working your way to the edges. You can also use a credit card to smooth it out.

* Let it dry for a few minutes then add another thin layer of Mod Podge over the picture.

* Once Mod Podge is dry, lightly paint the edges around the picture with black paint so it blends a little better (or you can just leave it how it is).

* Screw on the clock mechanism, put a battery in, and display the clock on the stand.

12. MAGNETIC BIRTHDAY CALENDAR

This is the perfect gift for a busy grandma to help her remember her grandkids' birthdays. If you use a different size magnetic board than called for here, adjust ribbon length and the spaces for each month's name accordingly. For the months-of-the-year stickers, feel free to use abbreviated or full-length names, but make sure the width of each sticker is no more than 2 inches so it will fit in the space provided on the board.

- 1 (18x18-inch) magnetic board
- Ruler or yardstick
- Pencil
- 1 (19-inch) ribbon
- Hot glue gun and glue sticks
- Months-of-the-year stickers
- Glass rocks with a flat side
- Scrapbook paper
- Scissors
- Sharpie
- Mod Podge
- Sponge paint brush
- Small round magnets

* Use a yardstick and pencil to mark a line that runs across the center of the board.

* Using the yardstick as a guide, align the ribbon straight across the board and attach it with double-sided adhesive tape.

* Using a pencil, make a mark above the ribbon every 3 inches for a total of 5 marks.

* Do the same below the ribbon. You should have 6 spaces above and 6 below the ribbon.

* In each space, center and secure a month-of-the-year sticker, starting with January. The first 6 months will be above the ribbon and the last 6 below it.

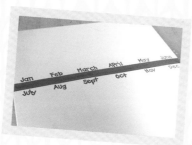

* Use one of the glass rocks to make a template on the scrap paper. Once the template is drawn, cut it out and trim the edges a little bit so when the rock is placed over the paper, the paper does not extend beyond the edges of the rock.

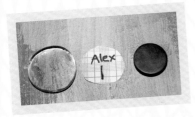

* Use the template to make and cut out enough papers for every name you will put on the birthday board.

* Write a person's name and the number of day he or she was born on each paper. Alex was born on the 1st, so his paper has the number 1 on it, along with his name.

* Paint a very thin layer of Mod Podge on each paper circle over the name and number. Quickly press the paper circle against the glass rock and smooth it out, starting from the inside and working outwards.

* Hot glue a magnet to the back of each rock once the papers have dried.

* Place each person's magnet under the correct month of their birthday.

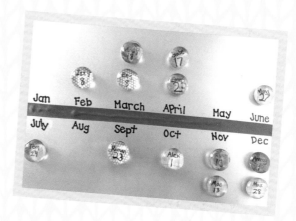

12
DIY
CHRISTMAS
DECORATIONS

It doesn't feel quite like Christmas until the tree is up and festive decor is adoring the house. Decorating your home can be expensive and time-consuming, but these decorating projects are affordable and are simple enough that the whole family can work on them together.

1. CINNAMON STICK CANDLES

It doesn't feel quite like the holidays until the house smells warm and welcoming! These cinnamon candles are the perfect way to decorate your home and keep it smelling wonderful.

- Adhesive strips
- Two 6-inch pillar candles
- Cinnamon sticks
- Ribbon or fabric strips
- Scissors

※ Roll your tacky strips into small balls and place them in a row along the center of each candle.

※ Press cinnamon sticks into adhesive strips around the candle.

※ Tie the ribbon or fabric strip around the candle.

2. DIY WOOD CANDLE HOLDERS

You could spend a fortune buying expensive candle holders for your fireplace mantel. Or you could hit up the craft or hardware store for some inexpensive wood spindles and post caps and make your own. If you have a saw and don't mind a little extra work, you could also repurpose spindles and caps from an old staircase, coffee table, or other piece of

furniture. Thrift stores and flea markets are the perfect place to find odds and ends that can be turned into something beautiful.

- Wood glue
- 2 flat, square wood post caps
- 2 flat, round wood railing post caps
- 2 wood railing spindles
- Paint
- Paint brush
- Fine-grit sandpaper

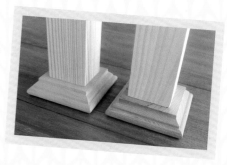

❋ Use the wood glue to attach 1 square post cap to the bottom of each spindle. Let dry completely.

❋ Glue 1 round post cap to the top of each spindle. Let the glue dry completely.

❋ Paint the candle holders with as many coats as you'd like, letting the paint dry between coats.

❋ Once paint is dried, use sandpaper to rough up the candlesticks a little and give them a distressed look.

3. PEPPERMINT CANDY WREATH

Add a festive touch to your front porch with this inexpensive DIY holiday wreath. If you live in a warm, humid climate, you may want to shellac the candies after gluing them to the wreath form so they don't melt and drip on your porch.

- 2 bags peppermint candies
- 14-inch styrofoam wreath form
- Hot glue gun
- Hot glue sticks
- Ribbon

* Unwrap the peppermint candies and set aside in a bowl.

* Hot glue peppermint candies to the wreath form to completely cover.

* Use ribbon to tie a bow on the top of your wreath and hang.

4. SEQUIN CHRISTMAS TREE

It wouldn't be Christmas without something sparkly! We know how busy things get during the holidays, but this is a cute decoration you can make even if you're short on time!

- Styrofoam cone
- Sequin ribbon
- Hot glue gun and glue sticks
- Felt
- Scissors

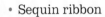

* Starting at the bottom of the cone, glue on one end of the sequin ribbon at a slight angle.

* Begin wrapping and gluing sequined ribbon around the cone.

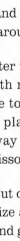

* After wrapping the entire cone with ribbon, lay ribbon across the top of the cone and secure in place with hot glue. Trim away any extra ribbon with scissors.

* Cut out a circle of felt the same size as the bottom of the cone and glue it to the bottom.

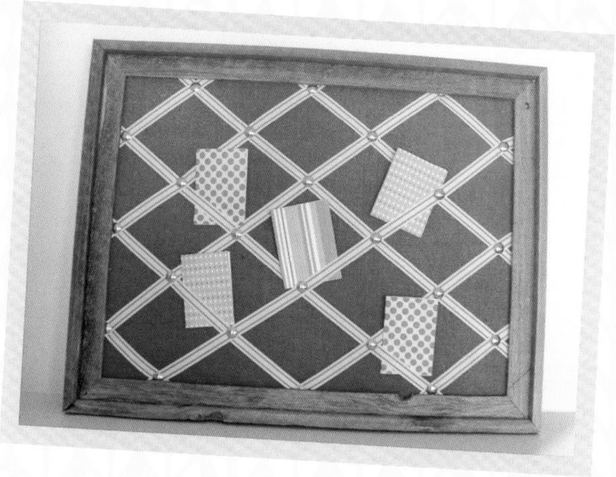

5. **CHRISTMAS CARD HOLDER**

This DIY card holder is the perfect way to display greetings from friends and family at Christmastime.

- 16x20-inch picture frame
- 1 square yard burlap fabric
- Quilt batting
- Scissors
- Staple gun and staples
- Ribbon
- Thumbtacks

❄ Remove glass, matte, and cardboard backing from the frame. Save the glass and matte for another project; keep the cardboard to continue with the next step.

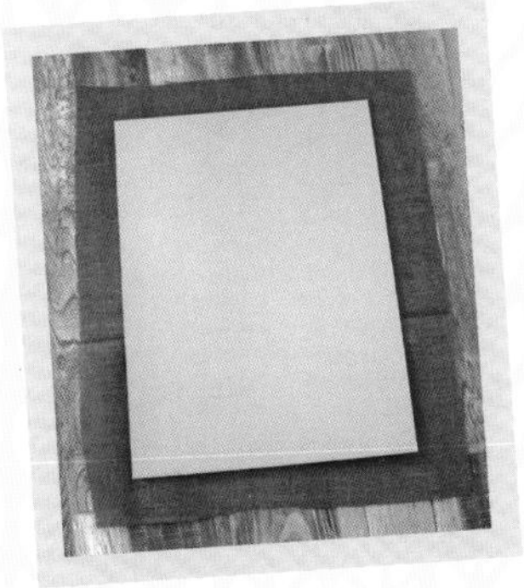

❄ Lay out fabric on a flat surface and place cardboard (from the picture frame) on top. Measure and mark fabric 3 inches around the edge of the cardboard on all 4 sides. Cut out fabric.

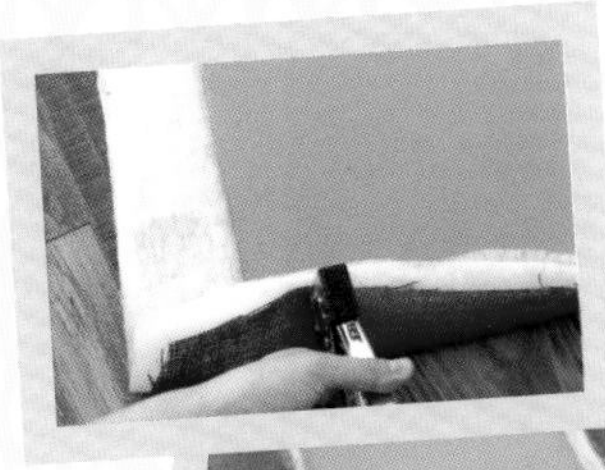

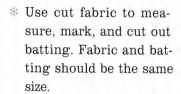

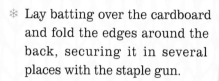

❄ Use cut fabric to measure, mark, and cut out batting. Fabric and batting should be the same size.

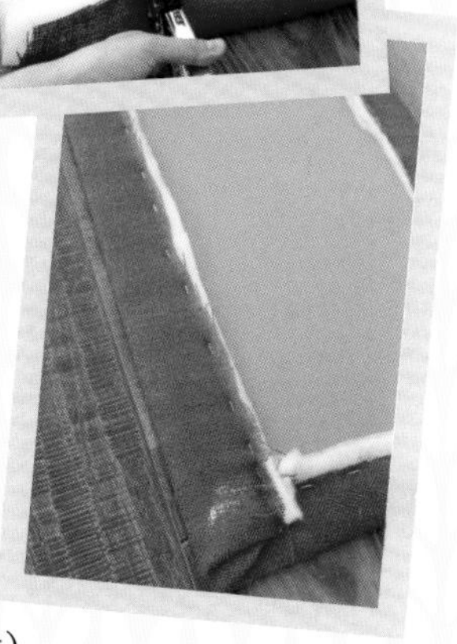

❄ Lay batting over the cardboard and fold the edges around the back, securing it in several places with the staple gun.

❄ Cover batting with fabric and fold the edges over the batting. Staple fabric (including the batting underneath it) around the entire piece of cardboard.

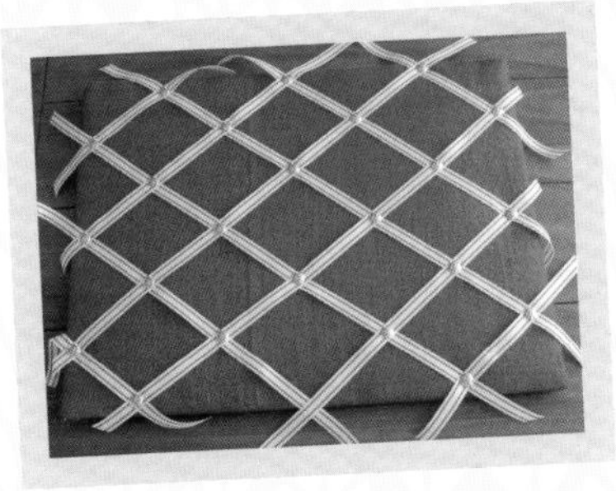

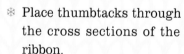

❄ On the front side of the fabric-covered cardboard, lay strips of ribbon to make a diamond pattern.

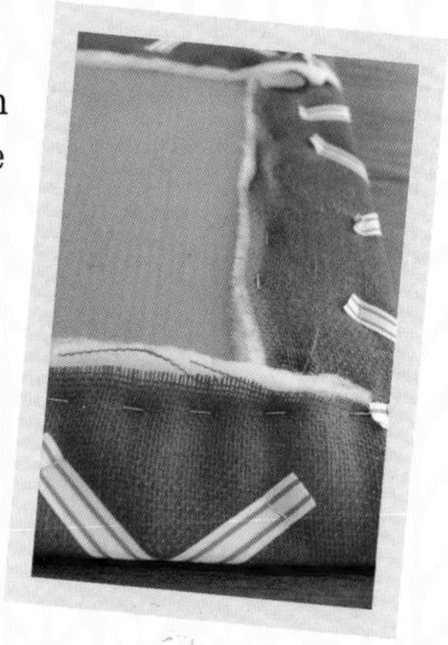

❄ Place thumbtacks through the cross sections of the ribbon.

❄ Flip the board over and staple the ends of the ribbon to the back of the board.

❄ Replace board in picture frame and display.

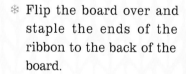

6. CHRISTMAS COUNTDOWN ADVENT CALENDAR

This is a simple and cute way to display a countdown calendar. If desired, you can purchase pre-cut circles at a craft store rather than cutting your own. You can also paint and distress the frame to fit your own décor.

- 3 to 4 sheets colored craft paper or cardstock (red, green, printed, or a combination)
- Scissors
- Foam number stickers, 1 to 24, in colors that coordinate with craft paper
- 24 (2¼x3½-inch) brown coin envelopes or similarly sized craft envelopes
- Glue
- 1 (16x20-inch) picture frame (may be larger or smaller, depending on size of envelopes)

- Wire
- Wire cutters
- Staple gun and staples
- Mini clothespins

❊ From craft paper, cut out 24 (2-inch wide) circles.

❊ Use the foam stickers to number each circle, 1 to 24, centering the numbers in the middle of each circle.

❊ Glue a numbered circle to the front of each envelope; set aside for glue to dry.

❊ Remove glass, matte, and cardboard backing from frame.

❊ Using the frame's width as a guide, measure and cut 4 pieces of wire slightly larger than the frame's opening.

❊ On the back side of the frame, staple each piece of wire from one side of the frame to the other to make 4 evenly spaced rows of wire. Wire should be fairly taut.

❊ Flip frame over and use the clothespins to hang numbered envelopes. Hang 6 envelopes on each row.

* On small pieces of paper, write something to do each day (visit a family member, sing Christmas carols, make cookies, and so on) and then slip each paper in an envelope. Let the kids take turns opening a new envelope each day!

7. CANDY CANE FRAME

This is a cute and easy decoration your kids can make to hold a picture with Santa or to give as a gift. You could also print out a fun design or Christmas saying to put in the frame.

- 1 (4x6-inch) wood frame
- White spray paint
- Roll of 1-inch painter's tape

- Red acrylic paint
- Paint brush
- Fine-grit sandpaper (optional)

* Remove glass, matte, and backing from frame.

* Spray paint frame white and let dry completely.

* Use painter's tape to create diagonal stripes across the frame. (Make sure stripes are the same width as painter's tape.)

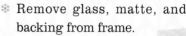

* Paint over the entire frame with red paint and let dry completely.

* Remove tape from frame.

* If desired, sand down edges and front of the frame to hide imperfections and give it a distressed look.

* Replace glass, matte, and backing.

8. MERRY CHRISTMAS CANVAS

Besides being a fun decoration, this is also a great activity for kids.

- 1 (9x12-inch) canvas panel
- 1-inch sticker letters
- Picture easel

✴ Lay out the letters on your canvas to make sure they are straight and begin and end where you'd like them. For example, if you want your text to be left aligned, put the letters on in reverse order to make sure they ended where you want them to.

✴ Stick on letters and place canvas on an easel to display.

9. POLKA DOT BURLAP TABLE RUNNER

We spend a lot of time at the table around the holidays, and cute table linens always help it feel more festive! This table runner is so simple to make that you don't even need a sewing machine!

- 12-inch roll of burlap
- Scissors
- Ribbon
- Yardstick
- Hot glue gun and glue sticks
- Paper
- Paper plate
- Red acrylic paint
- Circle sponge stencil

✴ Roll burlap fabric out the length of your table. Trim both ends so there is an overhang of 6 inches on each side.

✴ Measure and mark ribbon across the hanging end of burlap, adding an additional inch on each side. Cut two 14-inch strips of ribbon.

10. CHRISTMAS MONOGRAM HANGING

Monograms add a personal touch to the holidays. This craft is so simple and makes the perfect accent piece for your mantel, or even a cute decoration for your front door.

* Wooden monogram letter
* Green frayed jute
* Hot glue gun and glue sticks
* Decorative berries
* Ribbon

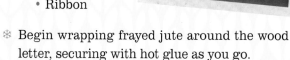

❋ Attach ribbon to the table runner using hot glue. Fold the extra ribbon over the edge of the runner and keep in place with hot glue.

❋ Place a piece of paper under the burlap to protect your table.

❋ Squirt paint onto a paper plate and then dip circle sponge stencil in red paint and stamp onto burlap.

❋ Begin wrapping frayed jute around the wood letter, securing with hot glue as you go.

❋ Continue to cover the burlap with polka dots, spacing evenly. Continue the entire length of the table runner. Let dry completely.

❋ Continue wrapping and gluing jute around the letter until it is completely covered.

❋ Lay decorative berries on the monogram where you want to attach them. Secure in place with a ribbon tied in a knot or bow.

11. FABRIC-COVERED DECORATIVE BOOKS

If you're looking for inexpensive pieces to add some color to your shelves or mantel, this project costs only a few dollars to make and will look darling anywhere in your home for the holidays. Shop at Goodwill or other thrift stores to get the old books.

- Hardcover books
- Fabric
- Scissors
- Spray adhesive

❋ Lay out the fabric and open the book flat on top of it.

❋ Cut the fabric 1-inch wider than the book on all sides when it is opened flat.

❋ Close the book and lay it on one side. Spray the other side and spine with spray adhesive.

❋ Quickly fold the fabric over the adhesive. Press firmly and run your hands over the cover to smooth out any bumps or wrinkles. Press along the spine to fit the fabric to the curves of the book. Repeat on the other side of the book.

❋ Open the book and then spray around the edge of the inside cover with adhesive spray.

❋ Fold fabric over, pressing down firmly. You may need a little extra adhesive in the corner where the fabric overlaps.

❋ Trim the fabric by the spine of the book down to a centimeter in length.

❋ Tuck the centimeter of fabric into the spine of the book. You can use a little spray adhesive to hold it in place.

12. CHRISTMAS ORNAMENT GARLAND

Fresh pine garlands are lovely, but they can get pretty expensive. If you have a lot of extra ornaments on hand, this is an easy way to make a colorful garland for your mantel or stair railing. You could also buy ornaments on clearance after Christmas and save them for next year to make this garland.

- Ornaments
- Twine

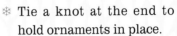

❋ Cut string or twine a few inches longer than the length of where the garland will be hung.

❋ String on ornaments until the entire length of twine is filled.

❋ Tie a knot at the end to hold ornaments in place.

INDEX

Page numbers in *italic* indicate images.

Advent Calendar, Christmas Countdown, 138–39
Almond English Toffee, *74*, 75
Almond Joy Bars, 82, *83*
Almonds
    Almond English Toffee, *74*, 75
    Almond Joy Bars, 82, *83*
    Slow-Cooker Cinnamon Almonds, 94
Andes Mint Grinch Cookies, *8*, 9
Angel Tree, Salvation Army, 90
Apple Pie, Dutch, *80*, 81
Apple Pie French Toast, Baked, *34*, 35
Applesauce Pork Tenderloin, 112, *113*

Baby Ruth Bars, *86*, 87
Bacon and Egg Breakfast Casserole, *30*, 31
Baked Apple Pie French Toast, *34*, 35
Balsamic Pot Roast, Slow-Cooker, *102*, 103
Banana Bread, Nutella, 40, *41*
Beans
    Chicken Taco Casserole, 120, *121*
    Slow-Cooker Chicken Fajita Soup, *106*, 107
    Slow-Cooker Texas Chili, *108*, 109
Beef
    Grandma's Meatloaf, 116, *117*
    Slow-Cooker Balsamic Pot Roast, *102*, 103
    Slow-Cooker Texas Chili, *108*, 109
Bell Peppers
    Bacon and Egg Breakfast Casserole, *30*, 31

Brunch Enchiladas, *50*, 51
    Slow-Cooker Ham and Pineapple Sandwiches, 100, *101*
    Slow-Cooker Texas Chili, *108*, 109
Beverages
    Frappé, 59
    Frozen Hot Chocolate, 56
    Warm Spiced Cider, *38*, 39
Birthday Calendar, Magnetic, 132–33
Black Beans
    Chicken Taco Casserole, 120, *121*
    Slow-Cooker Chicken Fajita Soup, *106*, 107
Bleach T-Shirts, DIY, 127–28
Blender Salsa, Easy, 95
Books, Fabric-Covered Decorative, 142
Books on CD, Personalized, 125–26
Bracelets, Hinge, 128–29
Breads
    Baked Apple Pie French Toast, *34*, 35
    Cherry Chocolate Muffins, *46*, 47
    Gingerbread Waffles, 36, *37*
    Gooey Caramel Pull-Aparts, *42*, 43
    Homemade French Toast Sticks, 44, *45*
    Homemade Orange Rolls, 32–33
    Homemade Waffles with Chocolate Hazelnut Sauce, 52, *53*
    Nutella Banana Bread, 40, *41*
Breakfast Casserole, Bacon and Egg, *30*, 31
Brownie Cookies, Double Chocolate, 90–91
Brownies, Rocky Road, 92
Brunch
    Bacon and Egg Breakfast Casserole, *30*, 31

Baked Apple Pie French Toast, *34*, 35
Brunch Enchiladas, *50*, 51
Cherry Chocolate Muffins, *46*, 47
Eggs a la Goldenrod, 48, *49*
Gingerbread Waffles, 36, *37*
Gooey Caramel Pull-Aparts, *42*, 43
Homemade French Toast Sticks, 44, *45*
Homemade Orange Rolls, 32–33
Homemade Waffles with Chocolate Hazelnut Sauce, 52, *53*
Nutella Banana Bread, 40, *41*
Warm Spiced Cider, *38*, 39
Brunch Enchiladas, *50*, 51
Budget, making and keeping, 55
Burlap Handprint Tree Skirt, 124–25
Burlap Table Runner, Polka Dot Burlap, 140–41
Butter Cookies, Gooey, 22, *23*
Buttercream Frosting, 3

Cakes
Mini Turtle Cheesecakes, 88, *89*
Pumpkin Pie Cake, 72, *73*
Calendar, Magnetic Birthday, 132–33
Candies
Almond English Toffee, *74*, 75
Double-Decker Fudge, *70*, 71
Homemade Peanut Butter Truffles, 97
Peppermint Fudge, 84, *85*
Candle Holders, DIY Wood, 135
Candles, Cinnamon Stick, 134
Candy Cane Frame, 139
Candy sled race, 58
Canvas, Merry Christmas, 140
Cape, T-Shirt Superhero, 123
Caramel Pull-Aparts, Gooey, *42*, 43
Card Holder, 137
Cards, digital, 56
Caroling, 59–60
Charity ideas, 90–93
Cheese
Bacon and Egg Breakfast Casserole, *30*, 31
Brunch Enchiladas, *50*, 51
Chicken Taco Casserole, 120, *121*
Slow-Cooker Chicken Fajita Soup, *106*, 107
Slow-Cooker Ham and Pineapple Sandwiches, 100, *101*

Cheesecake Cookies, Cherry, *4*, 5
Cherry Cheesecake Cookies, *4*, 5
Cherry Chocolate Muffins, *46*, 47
Chicken
Chicken Taco Casserole, 120, *121*
Slow-Cooker Chicken and Gravy, 104, *105*
Slow-Cooker Chicken Fajita Soup, *106*, 107
Sticky Sesame Chicken, *114*, 115
Chicken and Gravy, Slow-Cooker, 104, *105*
Chicken Fajita Soup, Slow-Cooker, *106*, 107
Chicken Taco Casserole, 120, *121*
Chili, Slow-Cooker Texas, *108*, 109
Chocolate Chips
Almond English Toffee, *74*, 75
Almond Joy Bars, 82, *83*
Baby Ruth Bars, *86*, 87
Cherry Chocolate Muffins, *46*, 47
Chocolate Chip Turtle Cookies, *12*, 13
Chocolate Orange Cookies, 10, *11*
Double Chocolate Brownie Cookies, 90–91
Double-Decker Fudge, *70*, 71
Frosted Toffee Cookies, 16–17
Peppermint Fudge, 84, *85*
Red Velvet Cream Cheese Cookies, 63
Rocky Road Brownies, 92
White Chocolate Macadamia Nut Cookies, 64
Chocolate Chip Turtle Cookies, *12*, 13
Chocolate Drizzle, 92
Chocolate Hazelnut Sauce, 52
Chocolate Orange Cookies, 10, *11*
Christmas Card Holder, 137
Christmas cards, digital, 56
Christmas Countdown Advent Calendar, 138–39
Christmas Monogram Hanging, 141
Christmas Ornament Garland, 143
Christmas Tree, Sequin, 136
Cider, Warm Spiced, *38*, 39
Cinnamon Almonds, Slow-Cooker, 94
Cinnamon Stick Candles, 134
Citrus-Glazed Salmon, 110, *111*
Clock, Photo, 131–32
Cookie Bars, Gingerbread, *66*, 67
Cookie dough, refrigerated, 94–95
Cookie exchange, 63

Cookies

Almond Joy Bars, 82, *83*

Andes Mint Grinch Cookies, *8*, 9

Baby Ruth Bars, *86*, 87

Cherry Cheesecake Cookies, *4*, 5

Chocolate Chip Turtle Cookies, *12*, 13

Chocolate Orange Cookies, 10, *11*

Double Chocolate Brownie Cookies, 90–91

Eggnog Cookies, 6, *7*

for heroes, 90

Frosted Toffee Cookies, 16–17

Gingerbread Cookie Bars, *66*, 67

Gooey Butter Cookies, 22, *23*

Grandma's Thumbprint Cookies, *20*, 21

Holiday Sprinkle Cookies, 1

Mint Chip Cookies, 18, *19*

Peanut Butter Snowballs, 68, *69*

Red Velvet Cream Cheese Cookies, 63

refrigerated cookie dough, 94–95

Santa Sugar Cookies, 2–3

Soft and Chewy Molasses Cookies, *14*, 15

White Chocolate Macadamia Nut Cookies, 64

Cream Cheese

Cherry Cheesecake Cookies, *4*, 5

Gooey Butter Cookies, 22, *23*

Mini Turtle Cheesecakes, 88, *89*

Red Velvet Cream Cheese Cookies, 63

Cream Cheese Cookies, Red Velvet, 63

Days of Christmas for Your True Love, 24–25

Decorating, as family, 54

Decorations

DIY, 134–43

organizing, 54

Decorative Books, Fabric-Covered, 142

Digital Christmas cards, 56

Dinners

Applesauce Pork Tenderloin, 112, *113*

Chicken Taco Casserole, 120, *121*

Citrus-Glazed Salmon, 110, *111*

for needy family, 92

Grandma's Meatloaf, 116, *117*

Perfect Fried Pork Chops, *118*, 119

Slow-Cooker Balsamic Pot Roast, *102*, 103

Slow-Cooker Chicken and Gravy, 104, *105*

Slow-Cooker Chicken Fajita Soup, *106*, 107

Slow-Cooker Ham and Pineapple Sandwiches, 100, *101*

Slow-Cooker Ham with Honey Mustard Glaze, *98*, 99

Slow-Cooker Texas Chili, *108*, 109

Sticky Sesame Chicken, *114*, 115

DIY Bleach T-Shirts, 127–28

DIY Wood Candle Holders, 135

Double Chocolate Brownie Cookies, 90–91

Double-Decker Fudge, 70, *71*

Drives, donating to, 93

Dutch Apple Pie, *80*, 81

Easy Blender Salsa, 95

Easy Infinity Scarf, 128

Eggnog Cookies, 6, *7*

Eggnog Gingerbread Trifle, 76, 77

Eggs

Bacon and Egg Breakfast Casserole, *30*, 31

Brunch Enchiladas, *50*, 51

Eggs a la Goldenrod, 48, *49*

Eggs a la Goldenrod, 48, *49*

Enchiladas, Brunch, *50*, 51

English Toffee, English, *74*, 75

Fabric-Covered Decorative Books, 142

Fake fudge, 96–97

Family gifts, 57

Family traditions, 26–29

Food drives, 93

Frame, Candy Cane, 139

Frappé, 59

French Toast, Baked Apple Pie, *34*, 35

French Toast Sticks, Homemade, 44, *45*

Fried Pork Chops, Perfect, *118*, 119

Frosted Toffee Cookies, 16–17

Frostings and Glazes

Buttercream Frosting, 3

Chocolate Drizzle, 92

Orange Glaze, 33

Simple Frosting, 1

Toffee Glaze, 19

Frozen Hot Chocolate, 56
Fudge
    Double-Decker, *70*, 71
    fake, 96–97
    Peppermint, 84, *85*

Garland, Christmas Ornament, 143
Gifts
    budgeting for, 55
    family, 57
    homemade, 122–33
    for neighbors, 94–97
    service instead of, 56
    white elephant gift exchange, 60
    wrapping, 55
Gingerbread Cookie Bars, *66*, 67
Gingerbread Trifle, Eggnog, 76, 77
Gingerbread Waffles, 36, *37*
Giving back, 90–93
Glass Vase Christmas Luminaries, 122
Gooey Butter Cookies, 22, *23*
Gooey Caramel Pull-Aparts, *42*, 43
Grandma's Meatloaf, 116, *117*
Grandma's Thumbprint Cookies, *20*, 21
Gratitude, expressing, 93
Grinch Cookies, Andes Mint, *8*, 9

Ham
    Brunch Enchiladas, *50*, 51
    Slow-Cooker Ham and Pineapple Sandwiches, 100, *101*
    Slow-Cooker Ham with Honey Mustard Glaze, *98*, 99
Ham with Honey Mustard Glaze, Slow-Cooker, *98*, 99
Handprint Tree Skirt, Burlap, 124–25
Headband, T-Shirt, 130
Heroes, cookies for, 90
Hinge Bracelets, 128–29
Holiday Sprinkle Cookies, 1
Homemade Christmas gifts, 122–33
Homemade French Toast Sticks, 44, *45*
Homemade Orange Rolls, 32–33
Homemade Peanut Butter Truffles, 97
Homemade Waffles with Chocolate Hazelnut Sauce, 52, *53*
Hot Chocolate, Frozen, 56

Ice Cream Pie, Peppermint Crunch, *78*, 79
Indoor snowball fight, 63
Infinity Scarf, Easy, 128

Light, as gift-giving theme, 96
Luminaries, Glass Vase Christmas, 122

Macadamia Nut Cookies, White Chocolate, 64
Magnetic Birthday Calendar, 132–33
Marshmallows
    Peppermint Fudge, 84, *85*
    Rocky Road Brownies, 92
Matches, as gift-giving theme, 97
Meal planning, 55
Measuring cups or spoons, as gifts, 96
Meatloaf, Grandma's, 116, *117*
Merry Christmas Canvas, 140
Mini Turtle Cheesecakes, 88, *89*
Mint Chip Cookies, 18, *19*
Molasses Cookies, Soft and Chewy, *14*, 15
Monogram Hanging, Christmas, 141
Muffins, Cherry Chocolate, *46*, 47

Neighbor gifts, 94–97
Nutella Banana Bread, 40, *41*
Nuts
    Almond English Toffee, *74*, 75
    Almond Joy Bars, 82, *83*
    Baby Ruth Bars, *86*, 87
    Baked Apple Pie French Toast, *34*, 35
    Chocolate Chip Turtle Cookies, *12*, 13
    Gooey Caramel Pull-Aparts, *42*, 43
    Grandma's Thumbprint Cookies, *20*, 21
    Mini Turtle Cheesecakes, 88, *89*
    Pumpkin Pie Cake, 72, *73*
    Rocky Road Brownies, 92
    Rolo Pretzel Turtle Bites, 95
    Slow-Cooker Cinnamon Almonds, 94
    White Chocolate Macadamia Nut Cookies, 64

Orange Cookies, Chocolate, 10, *11*
Orange Glaze, 33
Orange Rolls, Homemade, 32–33
Ornament Garland, Christmas, 143

Paper plates, 96

Party ideas, 58–65

Paying it forward, 91

Peanut Butter

    Baby Ruth Bars, *86*, 87

    Homemade Peanut Butter Truffles, 97

    Peanut Butter Snowballs, 68, *69*

Peanut Butter Snowballs, 68, *69*

Peanut Butter Truffles, Homemade, 97

Pecans

    Almond English Toffee, *74*, 75

    Baked Apple Pie French Toast, *34*, 35

    Chocolate Chip Turtle Cookies, *12*, 13

    Gooey Caramel Pull-Aparts, *42*, 43

    Grandma's Thumbprint Cookies, *20*, 21

    Mini Turtle Cheesecakes, 88, *89*

    Pumpkin Pie Cake, 72, *73*

    Rolo Pretzel Turtle Bites, 95

Peppermint Candy Wreath, 136

Peppermint Crunch Ice Cream Pie, *78*, 79

Peppermint Fudge, 84, *85*

Perfect Fried Pork Chops, *118*, 119

Personalized Books on CD, 125–26

Photo Blocks, Wood, 126

Photo Clock, 131–32

Pictionary, Play-Doh, 64–65

Pies

    Dutch Apple Pie, *80*, 81

    Mini Turtle Cheesecakes, 88, *89*

    Peppermint Crunch Ice Cream Pie, *78*, 79

Piñata, 60–62

Play-Doh Pictionary, 64–65

Polka Dot Burlap Table Runner, 140–41

Pork

    Applesauce Pork Tenderloin, 112, *113*

    Perfect Fried Pork Chops, *118*, 119

Pot Roast, Slow-Cooker Balsamic, *102*, 103

Pretzel Turtle Bites, Rolo, 95

Procrastination, 56

Progressive dinner, 64

Pull-Aparts, Gooey Caramel, *42*, 43

Pumpkin Pie Cake, 72, *73*

Race(s)

    candy sled, 58

    relay, 65

Recipe Binder, 131

Red Velvet Cream Cheese Cookies, 63

Refrigerated cookie dough, 94–95

Reindeer, Root Beer, 95–96

Relay Race, 65

Ring-and-run Christmas dinner, 92

Rocky Road Brownies, 92

Rolls

    as gifts, 97

    Homemade Orange Rolls, 32–33

Rolo Pretzel Turtle Bites, 95

Root Beer Reindeer, 95–96

Salmon, Citrus-Glazed, 110, *111*

Salsa, Easy Blender, 95

Salvation Army Angel Tree, 90

Sandwiches, Slow-Cooker Ham and Pineapple, 100, *101*

Sanity-saving Christmas Tips, 54–57

Santa's Helper, 59

Santa Sugar Cookies, 2–3

Scarf, Easy Infinity, 128

Sequin Christmas Tree, 136

Service

    ideas for, 90–93

    instead of gifts, 56

Sesame Chicken, Sticky, *114*, 115

Shopping, 55

Simple Frosting, 1

Slow cooker, using, 55

Slow-Cooker Balsamic Pot Roast, *102*, 103

Slow-Cooker Chicken and Gravy, 104, *105*

Slow-Cooker Chicken Fajita Soup, *106*, 107

Slow-Cooker Cinnamon Almonds, 94

Slow-Cooker Ham and Pineapple Sandwiches, 100, *101*

Slow-Cooker Ham with Honey Mustard Glaze, *98*, 99

Slow-Cooker Texas Chili, *108*, 109

Snow, shoveling, 93

Snowball fight, indoor, 63
Snowballs, Peanut Butter, 68, *69*
Soft and Chewy Molasses Cookies, *14*, 15
Soup kitchen, volunteering at, 93
Soups
    Slow-Cooker Chicken Fajita Soup, *106*, 107
    Slow-Cooker Texas Chili, *108*, 109
Spiced Cider, Warm, *38*, 39
Sprinkle Cookies, Holiday, 1
Sticky Sesame Chicken, *114*, 115
Sub for Santa, 90
Sugar Cookies, Santa, 2–3
Superhero Cape, T-Shirt, 123
Sweater contest, ugly, 62

Table Runner, Polka Dot Burlap, 140–41
Texas Chili, Slow-Cooker, *108*, 109
Thumbprint Cookies, Grandma's, *20*, 21
Tips, sanity-saving, 54–57
Toasting the season, 59
Toffee Cookies, Frosted, 16–17
Toffee Glaze, 19
Tomatoes
    Chicken Taco Casserole, 120, *121*
    Easy Blender Salsa, 95
    Slow-Cooker Texas Chili, *108*, 109
Traditions, family, 26–29
Tree Skirt, Burlap Handprint, 124–25

Trifle, Eggnog Gingerbread, 76, *77*
Troops, holiday treats for, 91–92
T-Shirt Headband, 130
T-Shirts, DIY Bleach, 127–28
T-Shirt Superhero Cape, 123
Turtle Bites, Rolo Pretzel, 95
Turtle Cheesecakes, Mini, 88, *89*
Turtle Cookies, Chocolate Chip, *12*, 13
12 Days of Christmas for Your True Love, 24–25

Ugly sweater contest, 62

Vase Christmas Luminaries, Glass, 122

Waffles, Gingerbread, 36, *37*
Waffles with Chocolate-Hazelnut Sauce, Homemade, 52, *53*
Walnuts
    Gooey Caramel Pull-Aparts, *42*, 43
    Grandma's Thumbprint Cookies, *20*, 21
    Pumpkin Pie Cake, 72, *73*
Warm Spiced Cider, *38*, 39
White Chocolate Macadamia Nut Cookies, 64
White elephant gift exchange, 60
Wood Candle Holders, DIY, 135
Wood Photo Blocks, 126
Wrapping gifts, 55
Wreath, Peppermint Candy, 136